Miss Manners'
Basic Training™:
Eating

MISS MANNERS'
BASIC TRAINING™

EATING

JUDITH MARTIN

CROWN PUBLISHERS, INC.

NEW YORK

Published by Crown Publishers, Inc., 201 East 50th Street, New York, New York
10022. Member of the Crown Publishing Group.

Random House, Inc. New York, Toronto, London, Sydney, Auckland
http://www.randomhouse.com/

CROWN and colophon are trademarks of Crown Publishers, Inc.

Printed in the United States of America

Design by Debbie Glasserman

Library of Congress Cataloging-in-Publication Data is available upon request.

ISBN 0-517-70186-3

10 9 8 7 6 5 4 3 2 1

First Edition

FOR THE KITCHEN STAFF AT CA' MINOTTO:
ROBERT, PANDORA, JEREMY, JANET, KATHRYN,
MICHAEL, NICHOLAS AND JACOBINA

Before beginning, Miss Manners would like to offer grateful thanks to David Hendin, Ann Hughey and Lucinda Williams.

CONTENTS

Miss Manners'
Basic Training™:
Eating

INTRODUCTION

Are we a society that doesn't know how to eat? Of people who can't manage successfully to get food of their own choosing into their own mouths?

Evidently. It is not so much observation that prompts Miss Manners to recognize this stupefying possibility: She is too polite to monitor others as she dines (a point of etiquette that calls into question why table manners are necessary at all, but she will ignore that). She has been astonished to hear from others that the skill of eating, according to our very own customs, once practiced at all levels of society, has all but disappeared.

It is not just tsk-tskers who report this, although there is ample nausea-ridden testimony from people who do observe others, either in the normal course of life or at posh job interviews. Countless people admit—although it sounds more like bragging—that they don't know how to manage a fork and that they dissolve into quivering helplessness when faced with a place setting consisting of more than one. Miss Manners is at least grateful that this rather basic failing has not resulted in the population's starving to death from being unable to figure out how to navigate nourishment on the perilous journey from plate to face. Yet an astonishing number of these people have been observed to be adept in using plastic flatware. It is no mean feat to attack a scoop of hard ice cream with a plastic spoon, or a respectable steak with a plastic knife and fork. So what seems to be the problem here?

Partly it seems to Miss Manners to be blatant know-nothingism. Pride in ignorance has never much appealed to her, and the usual form of this version, to which she is all too frequently subjected, makes her suspicious.

"What always panics me," the confessor inevitably says with an ingenuous smile, "is when I see five forks on the table and I don't know which one to use."

"Where was that? Where did you see those five forks?" Miss Manners inquires with a matching smile.

Nowhere, it always turns out. These people are never able to name a restaurant or dinner party featuring five forks at each place setting (a display which, by the way, would be against the rules of etiquette). At the most, they have seen three forks, but usually only two. Do they really mean to confess that they can't tell the salad fork from the meat fork? And worse, that not caring enough to learn, they nevertheless care enough to go to pieces?

Ignorance of eating skills is not a sign of lack of intelligence. It is more likely to be a sign of the sad demise of the family dinner. With the prevalence of refrigerator-grazing and fast-food-on-the-run among people of all ages, the skill of eating in a way that will not spoil the appetites of other diners is rarely taught. This includes the reasonably accurate use of proper utensils, an attempt at personal comportment and an acquaintance with the rituals for different kinds of meals in a variety of settings.

Here is a fast remedial course for those who have never learned, and a review for those who weren't paying close attention. It requires practice, but if there is one thing we have a chance to practice, it is eating. Few people have to be urged to practice this habit at least three times a day every day of their lives.

PLATE LICKING

DEAR MISS MANNERS—My husband's manners are appalling and frankly I am sick of it. When we have dinner at home, he starts eating and often finishes his dinner before everyone else is seated. When he has eaten the food on his plate, he scrapes it with his fork to get the last bits, and then he licks the plate. Yes, I mean with his tongue!

Since he is always still hungry, he brings pots from the stove to the table and eats from them, using the cooking utensils instead of his silverware. Once he has finished his dinner, he regales our young daughter with funny stories, thereby causing her to choke on her food. Then he abruptly retires to the television while we are still eating, leaving his pots and dishes in his wake. My husband is an educated professional man who uses excellent table manners in public. Why does he behave this way at home? How can I get him to improve?

GENTLE READER—Miss Manners is sick of your husband, too, and she hasn't even met him, much less broken bread with him. It is not only your vivid description of him at table that repels her, but also his attitude, which she has encountered before. It is the argument, highly insulting to his family, that he need not bother to consider the feelings of his own relatives as he does those of his business associates.

This is known as the privilege of being oneself at home. Why one would want to reveal such a self, or why anyone else would want to live with it, Miss Manners cannot imagine. However, it is hardly her job to go around wrecking families. She will endeavor to do the opposite.

Miss Manners suggests that you engage your husband in a gentle discussion about why he uses proper table manners in public. He will be unavoidably led into declaring that other people expect proper table manners and that he cannot afford to incur their distaste for his behavior.

That is the time to ask kindly whether the feelings of you, his wife, are not of even greater importance to him. He would have to be callous indeed to declare that he feels he can afford to arouse daily distaste in his own wife. Another point to bring up is that your daughter will be ill equipped to succeed in life if she, unlike him, does not even have the ability to exercise good manners when they are necessary to her professional and social welfare. Good manners are nearly impossible to teach while a parent is defying them. Miss Manners sincerely hopes that the appeal to his heart will prevail, without your having to appeal to the snobbery of success-seeking.

A NON–NEGOTIABLE RULE

DEAR MISS MANNERS—I have been trying to teach my two young grandsons a few of the graces I was taught at the dinner table, encouraging them to use the right knife, fork, etc., in the correct order; and to lay the napkin on the chair if one is coming back to the table, as in buffet dining, or to leave it on the table if one is not. They insist that I am making up rules as I go along and that these are not really etiquette.

GENTLE READER—Oh, they do, do they? Miss Manners suggests that you challenge them to put down exactly what they believe the rules of etiquette to be. You will either conclude the argument or end up with a nice little rule book that you can use to throw in their faces when they violate its tenets. But as "Never insinuate that your grandparents don't know what they are talking about" is a non-negotiable rule, they are going to have a hard time of it.

CHAPTER 1

EQUIPMENT AND ITS USE

THE BASIC IDEA

Everybody's favorite eating utensils are homegrown. Fingers are easy to wash, pose no confusion about which one to use and rarely get caught in the garbage disposal. Best of all, we each already own a more or less matching set.

Yet even fingers can be rudely used, and you kids cut that out right now. In addition to that misuse, lifting the littlest finger or two when holding a cup or a bone, which was an ancient symbol of refinement, turned bad about a century ago and is now the symbol of pretentiousness.

The first etiquette rule about finger food has to do with what is and what isn't. (For details, please see Chapter 2, Food Traps.) To deal with what isn't, it is necessary to be able to handle a few other technologically uncomplicated devices for getting hot, liquid or runny food into the digestive system. These are (pay attention—no blowing bubbles into your drink while Miss Manners is talking) the fork, the knife and the spoon, plus the napkin as insurance.

"Stuff it in whatever way you can" is not the rule governing the less formal means of obtaining sustenance. The etiquette of proper eating is not so snobbish as to assume that only people who can afford to patronize sluggish restaurants have sensibilities. Rules about alternating the two basic mouth functions of chewing and conversation are not suspended, no matter how fast one wants to get through both.

As a matter of fact, it happens to be more difficult to eat fast food than slow food. Slow food comes with many sturdy silver tools to help. What is difficult is not so much choosing among them, as reverse snobs think it comic to pretend, but making do without them.

How many of these implements one encounters at a time depends on how much food is being offered. Table-setting honor requires that no extra items be thrown in as a trick.

Utensils are properly placed in the order of their proper use, so the diner need only know to pick up those farthest from the plate on both sides for each course. With the exception of a skinny fork to be used for a first course of shellfish, forks may always be found on the left of the plate and knives and spoons to the right. That is to say that if the salad fork is on the outside, the salad is being served before the fish or meat; if it is on the inside, it is being served afterward. (Yes, you also have to know to pick the spoon for the soup, rather than the fork. Come on, folks.) Miss Manners urges the timid to take heart by realizing that if the amount of silver fails to match the number of courses, the table has been set wrong. There is no disgrace in asking for an inadvertently missing implement with which to eat.

The usual order of courses is oysters, soup, fish, entrée (not the term for a main course, no matter how many restaurants think so, but an interim dish, such as asparagus, sweetbreads or mushrooms), roast with vegetable, game, salad, sweets, cheese, fruit. Fortunately for the carpet, it is no longer usual to serve more than three (all right, five on all-out occasions) of these courses at one meal.

In an ideal place setting, forks and knives would be used in pairs. In real life, there are rarely salad knives or fish knives, so the orphaned forks must go it alone. Dessert silver should also come in pairs—a fruit knife and fork, or a dessert spoon and fork—but usually doesn't. If there is not a dessert service crossed at the top of the place setting and one is not brought in with the dessert, you use the fork or spoon that is left next to the plate.

In regard to the equipment for setting a proper table, there are two schools of thought:

1. Put out the exact tool for each item of food, and a few more besides. If etiquette bars you from playing with your food, it should at least allow other toys on the table.

2. A few basic, all-purpose items will do, the food not yet having been invented that can't be subdued by a simple spoon, fork and knife. And it's no crime if they don't all match.

Miss Manners has an idea that it may shock those who suspect the worst of etiquette to hear that the second attitude is, on the whole, the proper one. Dinner was never intended to be an obstacle course, and an overemphasis on gadgetry or on perfect sets is not quite nice because it draws attention to the expenditure involved.

Preferring tradition over panting consumerism, etiquette generally chooses the simple over the complex. It doesn't go so far as to pine for the eating habits of our early-nineteenth-century forebears, who speared whatever they could on the tips of their hunting knives and merrily poured everything else all over their faces. But it is wary of that mid-nineteenth-century diversification of silverware that led to a national panic over which fork to use. (And if modern thinking people are above such worries, Miss Manners would like to know why they persist in expressing that fear so long after most of the forks involved were melted down for their silver content.)

Bad News for Snobs

The ultimate test of table manners, the formal dinner party, isn't all that hard. A properly set table has the necessary flatware all lined up in order of use. This dinner will start with oysters (its little fork being the only fork to be placed on the right), followed by soup (you do have to know that soup is eaten with a spoon), and then (using the outermost forks and knives in turn) a fish course, the main course of meat or fowl, and then salad, perhaps with cheese. No more than three sets of forks and knives may properly be set out, so the implements with which to stuff down still more courses would have to be brought in with each.

The dessert silver could be placed above the top of the plate (fork closest and pointing right; spoon above it, pointing left), but here it will be brought in using a method that, although highly formal, requires guests to work. Issued a plate with fork and spoon on each side of a fingerbowl, the guest clears it by placing the fork on the table to the left, the spoon to the right, and the fingerbowl and its underlying doily to the left side. Refusing to cooperate results in getting sent to bed without dessert.

Drinking is easier, as it too often is, because the wines will be poured in proper order: sherry in the little glass in front, with the soup; white wine in the glass at right, with the fish; red wine in the center glass, with the meat; and champagne in the tulip-shaped glass, with dessert. The large glass at left is for water to go with aspirin after all that food and drink.

There is a serious etiquette breakdown pictured here, but it is unrelated to forks or glasses. Having abandoned the rule of talking first to the person on the right and then switching, halfway through dinner, to the person on the left, these selfish guests have left the poor stranded gentleman in the middle feeling like a fool.

Miss Manners feels a few pangs in acknowledging all this. If one is permitted a weakness in her line of work, it should be for peculiarly shaped silver thingamabobs. Truthfully, she does cherish that moment at table when her loved ones stare in disbelief at their place settings and ask what in the world she has found now. But it is key to this hobby that one admit to its outrageousness. If one rule of the table is to give everyone a fighting chance to attack all foods served without serious damage to body or wardrobe, an equally important one is not to scare away appetites.

Basic Flatware Skills and Manners

The fork is not a complicated instrument. Anyone who can figure out a modern telephone, not to mention a computer, CD player or fax machine, can properly manage a fork. In conveying food to the mouth, a fork or spoon is held the way a pencil is held, steadied between the forefinger and the middle finger, except that the thumb is turned up, rather than down as when one is writing.

When one is cutting food, the fork is held tines down in the left hand and the knife is in the right, each with an index finger firmly pressing down on the handle. One piece of food is cut at a time, and in the proper American style of eating, the knife is then placed back on the plate; the fork is transferred to the right hand and then lifted, with the food on top of the upturned tines, to the eager mouth.

The motion of scooping up food with fork or spoon,

whether it is soup or peas, is away from oneself. Miss Manners will allow you to guess why.

A METALLURGICAL ISSUE

DEAR MISS MANNERS—Can a fine quality of stainless steel flatware table service appropriately take the place of sterling silver for formal or very nice dinners in the home?

GENTLE READER—Etiquette is not in league with those who sell luxury goods to the carriage trade, however often the tradespeople who stand to gain may try to suggest this.

Not only does Miss Manners not endorse one metal over another, but she believes that anyone who too closely examines the value of any proper utilitarian tableware a host has set out is not paying proper attention to the conversation. And that comes from someone who can recognize an ounce's worth of difference halfway across an antiques show.

Does this sound like license to use plastic cutlery, even for an informal, let alone a formal, occasion? Forget it.

Miss Manners saved herself from that interpretation by inserting the word "utilitarian." Not liking to have fork tines break off into her dinner, she has not yet seen plastic flatware she considers utilitarian, and her mind, on that issue, is closed.

HANDS AND ELBOWS

DEAR MISS MANNERS—I was taught that one should eat with one hand in one's lap. Is this so?

I find it uncomfortable. At a sit-down luncheon, I looked

at everyone with their hands in that position. To me they looked like they all had broken arms.

GENTLE READER—Perhaps they did. This rule is often taught through brute force and there have been casualties.

A favorite method of instruction is gently to lift a child's arm and then drop it on the table, which sets the funny bone zinging. Children who are lucky enough to be out of reach may be warned ominously, "All joints on the table will be carved."

This may explain why even otherwise etiquette-free people remember this particular rule. It may also be why they remember it in an erroneously exaggerated form. The rule actually applies only to people who are engaged in eating. Those who lean forward for conversation between courses or after the meal are not violating the elbow rule, as vigilantes eager to pounce on them gleefully imagine.

This does not mean that Miss Manners is lax about the elbows-off-the-table rule for the irrelevant reason that it might make people uncomfortable. What makes her uncomfortable is the now-common sight of diners hunched over their plates as if to protect them from predators.

THE EFFICIENCY QUOTIENT

DEAR MISS MANNERS—My boyfriend the Engineer (industrial, not choo-choo) wants to know the reason why it is improper to cut more than one piece of meat at a time. He contends that it is not logical or efficient. It has become a bone (raw) of contention in our relationship, as I don't care about its origin. I just care that he exhibits proper etiquette.

GENTLE READER—Please tell your boyfriend the Engineer that Miss Manners the Etiquetteer wishes to disabuse him of the foolish notion that rules of etiquette are intended to be either logical or efficient.

Is eating with a fork and knife more logical than with chopsticks, or with the fingers? Why does he want to eat more efficiently—does his doctor complain that he is not shoveling it in fast enough?

Your attitude—not caring why but caring that things be done properly—is infinitely preferable. Etiquette is folklore, and folklore simply cannot stand that sort of cold scrutiny. We do things this way because this is the way we do things.

We cut only one mouthful of meat at a time. No doubt the origin has to do with the pre-Victorian habit of eating with the knife (cut and shovel in one gesture—your boyfriend would have loved it). And if you care to, you may argue that heat loss from the meat is proportional to the surface area. Miss Manners would prefer to think about something else during dinner.

EATING LEFT-HANDED

DEAR MISS MANNERS—Was my dear mother somehow remiss in allowing me to choose to use my left hand to hold my fork or spoon? I understand that many people, regardless of which hand they use for writing, were taught as children that the fork is always held in the right hand—even though it is placed to the left of one's plate.

When seated in close quarters with people using their right hands, I have tried to place myself at the end of the table to lessen the chances of bumping elbows. Should I have learned to use my right hand long ago, saving the worry of elbowing someone accidentally? I am afraid that if I were to switch hands now, I might be sloshing soup and dropping peas for a long time before I get the hang of it.

GENTLE READER—Miss Manners herself has no intention of splattering anyone, least of all your dear mother. While it is true that table habits are geared toward the right-handed majority, we should all be able to eat peacefully together with the hand of our choice, and without having to get up from the table to march for minority rights.

There are circumstances in which you can command a seat that is easy for you, but they do not include displacing a host or disrupting a seating plan. You might want to keep your elbow in just a little more, and as a matter of fact that applies to everyone. Miss Manners is tired of seeing flying elbows, no matter what route they take.

The other problem will be when you are required to serve yourself from a platter. Service is offered from the left so that the right hand is unconstrained. You need simply get it to your right side—by yourself if the platter is passed, or by asking a waiter to serve you on your right and then by getting to it before the person on your right grabs the serving utensils for himself. Although these procedures can be complicated by odd foods and specialized flatware, they are basic to any meal, and the rest can be extrapolated from it.

HISTORICAL FICTION

DEAR MISS MANNERS—Can you help me confirm or deny a story I heard about American eating habits:

American etiquette requiring that the left hand be in one's lap while eating originated during the Revolution. To protect themselves from potential British attack while they were eating, the colonists held a gun under the table in their left hand while eating with their right hand.

Is that true? If so, were the colonists all proficient in shooting left-handed? If it isn't true, why do Americans want to eat one-handed? It seems much more practical to follow the European etiquette and use both hands for manipulating eating utensils.

GENTLE READER—Miss Manners has heard a lot of weird stories purporting to connect etiquette rules with historical necessities, but she has to admit that this one is a gem. The thought of all those left-handed revolutionaries cradling guns while spooning up the soup is fascinating. It is too bad that pictures from the era don't document the arsenal under the dinner table.

Unfortunately, these stories are generally invented to explain existing differences. Miss Manners wonders if you have heard the common American explanation of why Europeans park their left hands on the edge of the table while eating, instead of in their laps, as we consider normal. It is because (the story goes) they do not trust one another to have their hands under the table.

AMERICAN AND EUROPEAN STYLES

DEAR MISS MANNERS—Is it acceptable in the United States to use the European method of dining with the knife in the right hand and the fork in the left, cutting the food as you eat it?

GENTLE READER—Is it acceptable for someone in the United States to speak with, say, an English or French accent?

Certainly, if that person is a foreigner or foreign-born. Eating European style (keeping the fork in the left hand and

Worse News for Snobs

The European method of keeping the fork in the left hand while eating is not more chic than the American method of switching the fork to the right hand after each bite of food—just different and good enough for them. When affected by Americans, it is pretentious and, in the case of the gentleman at right, perilous. If anything, the American way is snazzier because it comes from an older tradition, imported from Europe before Europeans figured out how to eat faster—not a charming goal, as we know from the even more efficient eating style of infants.

packing food onto the back of it with the knife) rather than American style (switching the fork to the right hand after cutting and bringing food to the mouth with the fork facing upwards) is acceptable in the United States for foreigners and the foreign-born. In anyone else, it is considered affected.

CHOPSTICKS

Chopstick usage varies in different countries, as indeed do the implements themselves. Here is the basic technique considered acceptable when practiced by westerners:

Chopsticks are held as if you were using two pencils at once, except that the lower one is gripped between the thumb, at about knuckle level, and the end of the ring finger, while the upper chopstick is gripped between the end of the thumb and the end of the forefinger, with the assistance of the middle finger. This should provide enough leverage to grasp food by moving the upper chopstick down so that the tips hold it securely enough to get it to the mouth without incident.

Of course, a lot depends on what we mean by "it." Grains of rice? Slippery noodles? Tiny tofu squares that collapse under pressure?

This may be the place for Miss Manners to mention that one may properly ask for a fork when dining in an Asian restaurant in the West—although they are usually already provided by restaurateurs, who have no desire to witness or clean up after ineptitude. Tourists attempting a difficult foreign custom should cultivate a look of appealing stupidity that will give their mistakes a sort of childish charm.

Things you may not do with your chopsticks include stabbing (food or people), putting the parts that have been in your

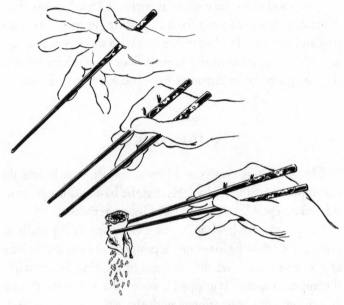

An East-West Trade-off

Although chopsticks prettily solve that dreaded problem of having to select which fork to use, they are harder to use, and not just for clumsy Westerners. Asian parents now grumble that the younger generation doesn't know how to eat properly. Sloppy Westerners are judged more kindly if they look apologetic and, when things get really out of hand, politely request a fork.

---

mouth into a communal bowl (Chinese restaurants provide a spoon to get around this practice, and the Japanese method is to reverse one's sticks), parking them in the bowl crossed or pointing across the table (they are left on a chopstick holder or on the paper container in which they came), or doing any of those other nasty things imaginative children of all nations come up with.

THE SOUP SPOON

DEAR MISS MANNERS—Where do you place your mouth and lips in relation to a soup spoon? A friend and I have a difference of opinion. I say you sip from the side, but if it's a thick type of soup with lots of items in it (such as pieces of vegetables), you place the tip of the spoon in your mouth so you can consume the liquid and whatever else at the same time.

GENTLE READER—Yours would be an excellent solution if the journey of food to mouth were merely a transportation problem, to be figured out on a practical basis. But if that were the case, Miss Manners would also have to listen to more efficient movers, who might point out that picking things out of the soup with the fingers would be even more practical, provided that the soup wasn't scalding.

One always pours soup, even goodie-laden soup, into the mouth from the side of an oval soup spoon. Perhaps Miss Manners can make up for this bad news by telling you about the gumbo spoon: It's large, it's proper for soups with a lot of things in them and it's round, so it is less obvious if you slip from side to tip.

EXTRA SPOONS (AND SOME PLATES)

DEAR MISS MANNERS—My boyfriend insists that when we are having company (unless it's a picnic), a spoon is to be set, along with whatever other flatware is needed, even when there is nothing being served that requires a spoon. The dinner in question consisted of green salad, grilled halibut, wild rice and bread. In addition, he felt that bread plates weren't necessary, as that created too many dishes on the table, in addition to dinner and salad plates.

GENTLE READER—Miss Manners appreciates the interest that both of you take in the properly set table and the opportunity she has to side graciously with both of you.

She is with you on the spoon. Contrary to popular fears, table settings are not tricks to humiliate people who can't see a relationship between the flatware and the food. The two are directly connected: What is set out is there to be used and is even placed (outside to inside) in order of use. A spoon is not set out unless it is needed—for grapefruit at breakfast, for example, or for soup at dinner. A dessert spoon would be placed above the plate, parallel to the table's edge. (Which reminds Miss Manners—you didn't have any dessert, did you? Are all your friends on diets?)

However, she is with the gentleman in thinking that three plates for each person would make the table look like a china shop. Bread can always be placed on the edge of the main plate, or on the tablecloth (yes, surprisingly enough—as long as there is no butter involved to make grease stains). You could also serve the salad as a separate course.

THE KNIFE

DEAR MISS MANNERS—My niece, an educated and charming person, holds her knife and fork in a most awkward fashion. She holds her knife completely vertical while cutting her meat. Please comment.

GENTLE READER—She tries to cut meat while holding her knife in a completely vertical position? The poor lady. She will probably starve to death.

PACKING THE FORK

DEAR MISS MANNERS—Is a person allowed to eat a small portion of potato and meat together from the same forkful of food, or must they always be consumed separately?

GENTLE READER—Making a food package on the fork, such as using mashed potatoes to cement meat and peas onto it, is considered distasteful in America—to other diners, that is. However, those who find it tasty may absentmindedly allow the prongs of a meat-laden fork to drift idly into the potatoes on its way to the mouth. Or they can learn how to park meat in a discreet corner of the cheek until the potato delivery arrives on the next fork run.

EATING WHILE TALKING

DEAR MISS MANNERS—Please discuss talking with a mouth full of food.

GENTLE READER—Ummm. Umghumghummm.
Translation: Can't talk now. Busy chewing.
Even after swallowing, Miss Manners can't make a discussion out of the question of talking with one's mouth full. It requires only one word, or possibly two:

1. Don't.
2. Yuck.

SPINACH IN TEETH

DEAR MISS MANNERS—This problem may seem trivial, even gross to young Miss Manners, but senior citizens really need to know what to do about food particles that lodge in the gumline and between the teeth and look terrible.

My dentist advises that with age, gums recede a bit, and teeth shift, creating spaces for bits of food to find a home. When dining with friends, I rarely smile for fear that my teeth may be holding bits of food—the old spinach-stuck-in-the-teeth problem. Should I secretly hold a mirror in my lap and glance down occasionally while smiling, thus giving the impression that I have a private joke or that I am just loony?

GENTLE READER—Given the choice between seeming glum and seeming loony, Miss Manners would go for the latter. Anyway, it would have to be a cheerless dinner party indeed for a mere smile to get people wondering about one's sanity. On the other hand, she is not suggesting that you beam food-ridden smiles around the room.

Intimates ought to be able to signal to you simply with a significant look and a fleeting gesture toward their own teeth. Others are required to express a face-saving element of doubt: "I can't quite tell, but there may be something on your tooth."

The mirror in the hand is a good sure way to check oneself. One would have to turn slightly away, anyway, to do a thorough search job with the tongue (without, of course, opening the mouth). A well-polished dinner knife could also be used if not brandished in a threatening manner.

The only other safeguard is a spouse or close friend within sight (the only good argument Miss Manners has ever heard for seating couples next to each other). Shooting a sudden smile at a loved one is heartwarming to observers, provided they only get a sideways view of it—even if the loved one's response is raised eyebrows and a quick negative nod.

REMNANTS IN THE TEETH

DEAR MISS MANNERS—I have insisted that dental floss, along with toothpicks, be readily available—in a smart container, not the commercial plastic boxes—should any guest desire it. I maintain that as long as it is proper to provide toothpicks at table, it should also be appropriate to provide the more efficient dental floss. Should we, where manners are concerned, be confined to the modes and mores of a previous century which lacked our marvelous technology? After all, dental floss is more thorough at cleaning the teeth and far less dangerous than wooden toothpicks.

GENTLE READER—Have you considered those technologically advanced devices that clean the teeth by shooting water into the mouth? Perhaps you could have some made in silver to go with your place settings.

It is a major flaw in your argument that you presume, erroneously, that toothpicks are proper on western dinner tables. Devices and maneuvers for the laudable hygienic purpose of cleaning the teeth, nose and ears are properly employed in private.

SIGNALING THE END

When one has finished a course, the implements used for it are placed across the plate, handles to the right (knife blade inward), in the approximate position of a clock saying 10:20.

A REPLY

DEAR MISS MANNERS—My wife assures me I misread your instructions about the proper placement of the fork and knife

in the 10:20 position. I have been placing my fork at the ten
o'clock position (assuming 12:00 is at the top center of my
plate from where I sit) and my knife at the 20 minute position (handles toward the outside of the plate of course!).

This leaves the dining implements 180 degrees opposed
from each other, with the sharp part of the fork touching the
knife blade. It does seem like a well-balanced arrangement that
should make it easy for a waiter or waitress to pick up the plate.

However, I have yet to observe one other individual do this,
despite the fact that I have dined with many people who I
would think should know proper etiquette. I have steadfastly
stuck to this habit at meals with fellow executives and, more
recently, at a wedding with my wife. If others all leave their
knife and fork in the 4:20 position, should I follow suit?

GENTLE READER—Playing with your fork and knife and with
your wife's and Miss Manners' nerves are all incorrect. And
4:20, for anyone as literal-minded as yourself, would put both
fork and knife handles incorrectly at the 10:00 position.

You have, however, convinced Miss Manners that she must
come up with a new comparison by the time digital watches
take over the world. In the meantime, stop having fun shocking people and put both handles at 4:00.

DESSERT AND COFFEE

Guests at fancy dinners may not be expected to bus their
own dishes, but they are not allowed to be idle, either. When
a formal dessert service arrives, consisting of a finger bowl on
a cloth doily, fork on the left and spoon on the right, the
diner is required to get busy—putting the fork on the table,
to the left of the remaining dessert plate, putting the spoon

on the right, and picking up bowl and doily and placing them to the left.

At this point you may, if you must, dip your fingertips (all of them—except that most people miss the little finger because it's too short—but not the thumb) into the water and wipe them on your napkin. Frankly, you haven't been eating with your hands at a formal dinner, so most people consider the finger bowl purely symbolic and skip the actual washing.

It is not absolutely required that you use both fork and spoon, and if you pick one, it should be the fork unless there is an obvious reason (a gooey dessert) to use the spoon. An unused utensil is left on the table. When you are using both, the fork remains in the left hand and the spoon in the right. This means that the fork is of little practical use, except possibly as a discreet pusher, but it is held on to nevertheless.

And what is the spoon with which dessert is eaten called? The spoon with which dessert is eaten is called a dessert spoon. Miss Manners threw that one in for extra credit and was astonished how many people thought that dessert should be eaten with a teaspoon. Presumably this mistake comes from silverware manufacturers, who sell the basic place setting as knife, fork and teaspoon, rather than the much more versatile oval spoon of greater size, which can be used for soup, dessert and cereal.

The teaspoon being used when tea is served, it is properly placed on the saucer of the tea (or coffee) cup. Thus it does not belong in a place setting ever, unless it is being pressed into service for something that is missing—in which case, one would have been better off buying the larger spoon at the same price.

PLATTERS

ASKING NICELY

DEAR MISS MANNERS—I believe that it is proper to use the word "please" when one is asking someone to do something—for example, "Please pass the potatoes." My mother-in-law seems to think that it is perfectly acceptable to do without the "please"—just "Would you pass the potatoes?"

GENTLE READER—Does anyone ever answer your mother-in-law by saying "No, as a matter of fact, I wouldn't?" or—considering that the person of whom such a bald demand is made happens to be armed with a plateful of potatoes—worse?

Those who lobby to drum out our pitifully few remaining forms of politeness should consider well what they are doing. In a world where no one acknowledged the polite necessity of being obliging to anyone else, no favors would be asked, but probably none would be offered, either. Does your mother-in-law really want to be at the mercy of the lucky person nearest the food, who has no incentive for yielding to her demand?

"SHORT-STOPPING"

DEAR MISS MANNERS—There is a recurrent argument in our family regarding what we describe as "short-stopping" at dinner. When a person is asked to pass something, should he first use whatever he is being asked to pass (e.g., salt or potatoes), or should he pass it directly to the person who asked?

GENTLE READER—Just pass it. Although this may require passing it back again, Miss Manners does not approve of a gesture that says, "Well, okay, but I get first choice."

DOUBLE-DIPPING

DEAR MISS MANNERS—A friend maintains that it is perfectly acceptable to dip a chip, take a bite, reverse the chip and dip again. He says that this is not double dipping. I say it is, even with the reverse of the chip, and not proper. Who is correct? We have a lobster riding on this.

GENTLE READER—It's worth a lobster because this happens to be a highly complex argument.

You are dealing only with the surface etiquette rule, which indeed states that one should not dip the same chip a second time. Meanwhile, your friend is dealing only with the manners principle that prompted the rule, stating that one should not put what has been in one's mouth back into a communal dish.

A true mastery of politeness consists of being able to reconcile the two. Tell your friend to break his chip in half before doing any dipping. He can then get just as much dip on his chip without dipping the same chip (or chip portion) a second time. Both of you should thus be able to enjoy your chips-and-dip, just as Miss Manners promises to enjoy the lobster you owe her.

FINGER LICKING

DEAR MISS MANNERS—Is there a tactful and gentle way to ask someone who is serving and handling food to stop licking their fingers after each serving?

GENTLE READER—Is this someone a professional server, your hostess, or your child who has been asked to help out at the table?

In the first case, you say, "I would prefer not to eat food that has been handled—could you please get me a fresh serving?" and, if necessary, complain to the management. In the third case, you say, "Stop licking your fingers, dear," and haul the child off for a hand washing.

The second case would be the hard one. The phrase you need then is, "No, thank you, I don't care for any more." You may also need to stop for a snack on the way home.

PAPER DOILIES

DEAR MISS MANNERS—Is it necessary to cover the bottom of a tray, plate or platter with paper doilies when serving sandwiches, cakes, cookies or sliced meat? I have also seen them used on a plate when serving a dish of ice cream or even a cup of coffee. I have always secretly thought this tacky, but it seems everyone but me uses them.

GENTLE READER—Dangerous is the word Miss Manners would use about doilies. She once watched in horror as a real doily was consumed at a candlelight dinner along with a chocolate mousse that the diner must have thought unusually chewy.

But even if placed a safe plate away from the actual food, paper doilies strike Miss Manners as affected and silly. The charming use she knows of is when little children make them into decorative snowflakes or valentines.

BUTTER-PAT PLATES

DEAR MISS MANNERS—I received a set of eight individual butter-pat plates (silver-plated, $2\frac{7}{8}$ inches in diameter) as a gift. Would you please advise me on how to use them correctly? At breakfast? Luncheon? With or without bread plates and butter knives?

GENTLE READER—Because she shares your delight in cluttering her table with dear old-fashioned oddities that others have forgotten, Miss Manners is delighted you will put this present to good use. She is also sorry to tell you that you cannot put them on the same table as bread-and-butter plates.

Bread and butter are not served at formal dinners, but they are at formal luncheons, where your little plates would be charming with, if you want to keep collecting, their own tiny butter knives. Technically, they need not be banned from breakfast or informal dinners, but those who plan to slather a big hunk of bread are not going to be satisfied with the wee pats or curls they hold.

COMMUNAL BUTTER

DEAR MISS MANNERS—A restaurant where we recently enjoyed lunch set a bread plate and an individual butter knife for each guest. Everyone used the individual knife to transfer butter from the butter dish to the bread plate. However, after seeing my friends fiddle with their butter knives on their bread, I felt compelled to resort to my dinner knife to spread my butter. My mother feels that using a butter knife for both serving and spreading is correct when an individual butter knife is provided for each guest.

GENTLE READER—In an ideal world, there would be a butter spreader, or butter pick, which each diner could use to transfer butter from the communal dish to the individual bread-and-butter plate. In restaurants, we all do the best we can.

Miss Manners is puzzled as to what seems to disgust you about knowing that the same butter knife that was in the common butter was also used to butter bread. Most restaurants serve butter in individual pats, rather than molds, and anyway, it isn't as though your friends were licking their knives. Is it?

SUBDUING BUTTER

DEAR MISS MANNERS—For years I have been trying to find out why there is a notch in the small knife served with rolls on a butter dish.

GENTLE READER—What you have is a butter server, notched in order to frighten and subdue recalcitrant pats of butter that are hoping to evade their fate. You may use it to stab them into submission for transport from the common butter dish to your individual plate.

By the time they arrive on your butter plate, they are presumed to have no more fight left in them. Therefore, a butter spreader, which is a benign-looking small knife with a rounded blade obviously not intended for combat, is then used to butter the bread.

GLASSES AND CHINA

For someone who goes mad with joy whenever she unearths yet another silver implement designed for the express purpose of eating one particular food—a joy that is undiminished by the fact that the food is extinct or is one she never liked in the first place—Miss Manners is amazingly liberal about glasses and china. If you slosh the burgundy into the claret glass, she'll toss it down without a qualm, and if the same plates pass themselves off as bread-and-butter plates at lunch, tea plates in the afternoon and fruit plates at dinner, all she asks is that they bathe between meals.

This devil-may-care attitude may be connected with the ephemeral quality of such objects. One small earthquake, or one attempt to push those glasses back a bit to make more room in the cupboard, and it's all over. Silver, on the other hand, is forever, or at least it will be once we get the crime problem under control.

From the point of view of the person doing the eating and drinking, the rules are simple. Any auxiliary plates you find to your left are yours; any drinking vessels to the right are yours. Even at the most formal meals, the necessity of eating from plates in the order they are put in front of you, and drinking wines in the order that they are poured during the meal, is grasped instinctively. But how much equipment does one need to put out to serve a decent meal?

GLASSES

It is possible to provide different glasses for water, sherry, chardonnay, hock wines, white burgundy, red burgundy, bordeaux, claret, champagne, port, cognac, brandy and liqueurs, and an endless number of cocktails, in addition to beer, punch, iced tea, soft drinks, juice and milk, but Miss Manners wouldn't classify that as decent. A water glass and one wine glass or milk or juice glass is decent; water and two wine glasses are considered positively festive.

For state occasions, five stemmed glasses per person is considered the maximum, and even that is pushing it. The sherry is nearest the knife, where it can be reached during the soup course, and the champagne glass (which it is wise to be wary about draining with the dessert in case anyone makes a toast) is in back. Curling above the knife are, from left to right, water, red wine for the meat course and white wine for the fish course. The water is for dabbing surreptitiously at the spots made on the tablecloth by knocking over one of the other glasses.

Aside from the Y-shaped sherry glass and the fluted champagne glass (or the saucer kind, which is not considered chic but can double to hold desserts), what is needed here are simply three sizes distinguishable from one another: large for water, medium for red and small for white; or only two, a water glass and an all-purpose wine glass. Unstemmed glasses come in short (for fruit juice or whiskey straight up, depending on the drinker's age, diet and mood) and tall (for mixed drinks, milk and diet soda—or regular soda; Miss Manners has begun to think of dietsoda as one word).

GLASSES VS. GOBLETS

DEAR MISS MANNERS—Many of the ladies enjoy wine coolers. On the patio, I serve them in regular water glasses. Inside, or on more formal occasions, I serve them in water goblets. Is that proper?

GENTLE READER—It's fine with Miss Manners: On the patio, they are an advanced version of iced tea; at the table, they are a retarded version of wine. She congratulates you on understanding the importance of context.

CANS

DEAR MISS MANNERS—While wine glasses and even coffee cups are practically useless for my generation, soda-pop cans don't look nice on a table set with linen and fine china. Almost no one in our circle drinks wine with dinner, a few drink tea, only two ever drink coffee, and the majority of our guests drink soda-pop or milk with dinner. Is my crystal passé?

GENTLE READER—As delighted as Miss Manners is that you want to use the lovely wedding present your Great-Aunt Tilly gave you, she does not want you feeling that you have to choose between that and your guests' happiness. You can have both.

What you cannot have is soda cans on the dinner table. Fortunately, although you should not do a drink less honor than it deserves, you can do it more. Thus, while wine should not be put in milk glasses, milk or soda would be thrilled to be put in wine glasses.

STEMWARE

DEAR MISS MANNERS—I would like to know the proper way to hold a stemware wine glass.

GENTLE READER—If etiquette went in for easy, smartsy answers, Miss Manners would say, "By the stem—isn't that what it's there for?"

Fortunately, etiquette is better behaved. So your question—which rightly presumes that the issue is more complicated—will get the respect it deserves. Stemmed glasses containing cold drinks are properly held by the stem. Those holding drinks served at room temperature may be warmed by the hand grasping the glass at the bottom of its bowl.

STRAWS

DEAR MISS MANNERS—When sipping a drink through a straw, is the glass left on the table, or picked up each time one takes a sip?

GENTLE READER—Pick it up. The exercise works off the calories from the drink.

EATING WHILE SIPPING

DEAR MISS MANNERS—Is it socially acceptable to take a sip of one's beverage with food in one's mouth, or should one wait until the food is swallowed before taking a drink?

GENTLE READER—There is no rule against sipping water while hiding food in the mouth; however, there is a rule against opening a mouth containing food. So unless you're planning to pour it up your nose (and if there isn't a rule against that, there will be the minute you try it), Miss Manners doesn't see how you are going to manage.

(For further elaboration, please see Fire!, page 152.)

CHINA

China is available in service plates, dinner plates, luncheon plates, oyster plates, fish plates, game plates, salad plates, dessert plates, fruit plates, tea plates and bread-and-butter plates. Also, bouillon cups, cream soup cups, rimmed soup plates, cereal bowls, tea cups, coffee cups and demitasse.

Fortunately, all these plates translate into large (main course at dinner), medium (breakfast, luncheon, fish and other early courses as well as, on the small side of medium, salad and dessert) and small (bread and butter, fruit and tea).

The small plates can also serve as underliners for cups and bowls: the two-handled small cups for bouillon, the larger two-handled cups for cream soup, and the modern all-purpose bowls that can be used for all soups, cereal and yummy sloppy desserts. Formal dinners require rimmed soup plates, in which clear soups are served because there's so much other fattening stuff yet to go.

Cups with one handle are coffee cups (not large, but the largest of this group), tea cups (medium) or demitasse. Of course, they could also be chocolate cups, which are small with straight sides, or broken bouillon cups. The only time cups belong on the table is for breakfast, when you are more likely to be using mugs with silly sayings on them, anyway. At lunch, they may be brought in after the meal or, as with demitasse after dinner, served away from the table after the meal.

Otherwise, we have a more or less sensible pattern of starting with small objects for breakfast, when that's about all one can handle, working up to medium for lunch, and going whole hog, as it were, for dinner.

FAMILY CHINA

DEAR MISS MANNERS—I have a question relating to the propriety of using chipped and worn dishes and serving pieces at dinner parties. Is it acceptable to set a table for guests with a few small chips showing in the dinnerware (but not the glassware)?

Some years ago, we would never have dreamed of doing so, but with time there is more and more damage and erosion. The items in question, acquired 25 to 30 years ago when we first set up a household, have become prohibitively expensive or un-available. We are far from being poor, but their replacement value has gone up much more rapidly than our income.

GENTLE READER—Miss Manners is of the school that deli-cately shuns anything too obviously new and perfect. Provided that your plates are not in danger of chipping off in the food, snagging anyone's fingers or giving up during the middle of a meal, Miss Manners classifies them as the family china, which, in a genteel family, looks used.

SERVICE PLATES

DEAR MISS MANNERS—I am confused by the variations I have seen in the use of service plates. At lovely dinners in the homes of friends and in fine restaurants, the person serving the meal seems to have discretion about which courses are served atop the service plates, and when the plates are placed on the table, and when they are removed from the table.

GENTLE READER—Technically speaking, all forms of service are at the discretion of those serving the meal, but observing what they do nowadays would generally be a poor guide to propriety. (Pay no attention to this unpleasant outburst, for which Miss Manners apologizes. It really has nothing to do with you or your friends or the restaurants you patronize; they are obviously making an effort, or they wouldn't be using ser-vice plates, which are a refined, but not obligatory, addition to the table. In their absence, the dinner plates to be used for the main course take their place. Miss Manners is just tired of mealtime sloppiness in the name of choice.)

But of course there are rules:

The service plate (also called a place plate, or a charger, a term Miss Manners reserves for knights on horseback or waiters with bills) can be made of china or metal, such as silver, pewter or brass. It is properly in place when the diners come to the table. The napkin may be centered on it, with a place card centered on that, in which case the diner (not the server!) removes the napkin for use and puts the place card aside.

One does not eat from the service plate directly. Soup plates, with or without underliners, are placed on the service plate; soup cups, used for luncheon, require underliners even when a service plate is used. Plates of oysters or clams are also put on top of the service plate.

The service plate is removed after the shellfish and/or soup course so that a plate for the fish or meat course may be substituted. This is done by having the server stand behind the diner, lean to the right to remove the service plate from that side, and then immediately lean to the left to slip in the fresh plate. This tricky maneuver, which makes the hair stand up at the back of a self-conscious diner's neck while it is performed, is done because at no time during a proper dinner, until just before dessert service, should the place in front of the diner be empty. Therefore, if no service plate is used, the actual dinner plate takes its place, with the difference that it is simply left there to be used for the main course when the early courses are finished.

As Miss Manners has mentioned that a service plate could be made of china, you may well ask what the difference is between a plate used as a service plate and a plate used for the main course. Well, it could have a different, more elaborate pattern, but frankly there needn't be any difference. You would just need twice as many of them.

ROTATING THE PLATE

DEAR MISS MANNERS—At mealtime in my own home, I have developed the habit of rotating my dinner plate in order to secure a better angle at which to pick up or cut whatever I am about to eat. I never thought much about it until one night at a dinner party, when the lady on my left tittered. I looked at her, and she said, "Well, why not?" Is rotating your plate merely a harmless personal eccentricity, a faux pas, or a hanging offense?

GENTLE READER—We don't allow eccentricities at the dinner table. Other people's digestive systems may become involuntarily involved.

Mind you, Miss Manners is not declaring this a hanging offense. Unless, of course, she finds herself mesmerized by your rotating plate to the point of involving her own lunch. Or if the plate has a crest which would be set askew. Rotating is not a good idea, however. Neither is employing table manners at home that cause titters when you are dining out. Technically, what you do that no one sees cannot be a violation of manners, but those who have to remember to eat differently when observed are making life unnecessarily difficult for themselves.

BREAD–AND–BUTTER PLATE

DEAR MISS MANNERS—If there is a bread-and-butter plate next to your dinner plate, should you use it for extras, such as applesauce or coleslaw, when these foods are served as condiments with the meal? Or is it correct to spoon them directly onto your dinner plate?

GENTLE READER—Miss Manners has trouble with applesauce and coleslaw being condiments. Maybe applesauce to go with a pork chop—but if it were on the bread-and-butter plate, it wouldn't be with the pork chop. She has even more trouble with the idea of such sloppy foods occupying a small plate. The bread-and-butter plate was intended for bread and butter.

DRINKING OUT OF THE BOWL

DEAR MISS MANNERS—A very close friend drives me crazy because he drinks out of a bowl. For instance, after eating cold cereal, he drinks the milk. He's the same way with soup. I was always raised that you finish what you start—with a spoon. He says he read it in an etiquette book. I say, show me the book. Suddenly he can't remember which one.

GENTLE READER—One possibility is that the gentleman has confused the delicately two-handled cup, used to serve bouillon, with the conventional bowl. The handled cup may indeed be properly lifted to the lips, but bowls, such as are used for heartier soups and for cereal, may not. (Please see Soup, page 62.) Another possibility is that he has been reading an etiquette book directed at cats.

TABLE LINENS

The size gradation used with china even applies to napkins, sort of: small for breakfast, medium for lunch and flag-size for dinner. (Teensy napkins are for holding cold cocktail glasses and sneakily hiding nonedibles, such as pits and toothpicks, that have no business accompanying hors d'oeuvres.)

If the napkin is not placed on the plate when dinner begins, it should be placed to the diner's left. This is one of those points that people love to deride as trivial—until they reach for a napkin and it isn't there because the person on the left reached for the right and the person on the right reached for the left. Then they discover that finicky Miss Manners has a point. It is no trivial matter to have to eat dinner unaided by a napkin, locked between two people of whom one is highly suspicious.

Table linens also gather force as the day goes on: place mats for breakfast, mats or modest tablecloths for lunch or informal dinners, and cloths at dinner that hang a good foot over the side of the table and that no one can even pretend to be able to iron without the fold marks showing.

Perhaps the main point to be made about table linens is that there should be some, and paper doesn't count. (Miss Manners fails to find logic in the notion that linens are a luxurious frill while their inadequate paper substitutes are somehow egalitarian.) Only when everybody's table manners are so perfect that nothing ever needs mopping up will Miss Manners be willing to argue that point.

MOPPING UP

DEAR MISS MANNERS—Cloth napkins are the problem. It is nice to have them on the lap while one is eating, but it is unpleasant to get sticky fingers and to have to use the napkin and then put it down on one's lap.

Since finger bowls are out, I have met the problem in my own way—a small moist towelette inconspicuously kept on my lap. However, these are not attractively packaged. It would be nice to have them tucked into the napkin as part of the table setting.

GENTLE READER—Just a minute here. Cloth napkins are not the problem. The job they do absorbing ordinary food messes puts any paper pretenders to shame, and not just for ecological reasons. It is not the napkins' fault that they need special assistance to handle the quart of barbecue sauce you tried to transfer from your spareribs to your own ribs.

So although Miss Manners appreciates your attempt to enter the etiquette trade by identifying problems and proposing solutions, she believes you will do better in this line if you think things through before assigning blame. People get their fingers sticky by eating with their hands; they do not come to the table sticky from spending the day mending old china with superglue. Therefore, a towelette, as you call it, would be useless tucked into the napkin at the beginning of the meal.

What you need is something to appear between a finger-food course and a course eaten with flatware. This is why the finger bowl was invented, in the days when fingers outnumbered flatware more than two to one. Many people still use finger bowls, either for practical reasons or out of ceremonial tradition, so you will oblige them, as well as Miss Manners, by not pronouncing them "out."

Paper trash does not belong on the table; if by "towelette" you mean a commercially packaged wiping tissue, you should refrain from using it. But you may certainly bring out small moist cloth towels, pleasantly warm at the time of use, after the messy course is completed.

NAPKIN RINGS

DEAR MISS MANNERS—My fiancée and I disagree on the frequency of changing cloth napkins on our dinner table. I say if the napkin is not excessively dirty or used to the point that it is obviously time for a change, it is proper to fold one's own napkin, place it in one's own napkin ring, and reuse it the following evening. (At a minimum, the napkin should be washed on regular washdays.) My fiancée insists on changing the cloth napkin every night. What is proper?

GENTLE READER—Napkin rings owe their existence to the practice of skimping on laundry that you describe. That was their function; any charm or beauty was incidental. You might point out to your fiancée that the carved silver napkin rings one sees at a decorative-arts museum or antiques show testify to the fact that those who could afford to employ a laundress and even aesthetically sensitive people succumbed to this practicality. Using napkin rings at dinner parties, as one sometimes sees now, would have been unthinkable.

No one ever argued that changing napkins with every meal was not an even better practice, provided someone else could be found to do all that washing. Miss Manners congratulates you on a fastidious fiancée, and on a marriage in which it is already clear whose chore the laundry will be.

INTERLUDE WITH A NAPKIN

DEAR MISS MANNERS—What should one do with the napkin if one must leave the table during a meal but will be returning? I heard that you put your napkin on the table, left side of the dinner plate, if you are returning. And you put your napkin on the table, right side of the dinner plate, if you are not returning. My brother believes you should put your napkin in your chair if you will be returning to the table. This topic comes up in my family every birthday and holiday dinner and it would be fun to have the answer for next time.

GENTLE READER—Next time, take your napkin and wave it frantically above your head. This has nothing to do with whether or not you are leaving or returning to the table, or any other kind of manners. Miss Manners is only suggesting it as the signal of surrender to your brother, to whom you have lost the argument. He is correct.

NAPKIN AS HANDKERCHIEF

DEAR MISS MANNERS—My nomination for the grossest table manners of the year: those of the person who uses a table napkin as handkerchief, then places it on top of the table when leaving. Can you or your readers think of anything worse?

GENTLE READER—Miss Manners is sure they can, so please don't encourage them. She has already thought of one herself: In rules of etiquette associated with George Washington (because they exist in his teen-age handwriting, although he was only copying earlier work) there appears, as rule 100, "Cleanse not your teeth with the Table Cloth Napkin Fork or Knife but if Others do it let it be done w/t Pick Tooth."

This, of course, means that people were commonly cleaning their teeth with the tablecloth then; if it had never occurred to anyone, there would have been no necessity for an etiquette rule prohibiting it. See what you've done?

CHAPTER 2

FOOD TRAPS

An innocent from New York City once thought to have a bit of fun discomfiting Miss Manners. Rather than inviting her to lunch at the sort of Washington pish-posh establishment to which this lady imagined Miss Manners to be accustomed, she chose a simple crab house as the place to enter into a discussion of etiquette.

In no time at all, Miss Manners was merrily pounding away with a wooden mallet, nabbing those crabs as they lay sprawled on a table covered by newspaper, prying them open by their own little beer can–like tabs, and having herself a fine old time. Her hungry hostess was reduced to begging for etiquette assistance, while using the unfortunate excuse that "You see, we don't have hard-shell crabs in New York—only soft-shell ones."

Miss Manners was happy to provide instruction in both etiquette and biology, and too polite to point out the other obvious lessons:

That etiquette covers the act of eating all kinds of foods, including marvelously messy ones—not just overpriced little morsels in pretentious establishments (which Miss Manners avoids when she can, as they are rife with etiquette errors, from rude attitudes to mis-set tables, while crab houses tend to know what they are doing, and to do it in a kindly spirit).

That the hardest thing etiquette requires is not eating, but refraining from laughing triumphantly when another is hoist by her own petard.

That it is neither easy nor wise to set a trap for Miss Manners.

Here are ways out of some common food traps:

Applesauce. As a dessert, it is eaten with a dessert spoon. Applesauce served with a main course is sneakily shoved on top of a bite of meat so that it doesn't fall through the tines of the fork.

Artichokes. This is the classic case where you must abandon your instincts, if you can even muster any, and admit that etiquette simply has to be learned, not deduced from first principles. Each leaf is pulled off, dipped in the sauce and silently pulled through the teeth. When the leaves are all gone, it is necessary to bring in reinforcements, in the form of a knife and fork, to scrape the prickly part off so that the heart may be eaten. Failing to do so, or attempting it with the fingers alone, carries its own punishment.

Asparagus. A thrill for the truly refined is to eat something properly, but in a way that those not aware of the nuances assume to be outrageous. Asparagus is born for this job. It may properly be picked up in the fingers, even under the most formal conditions, provided it is not limp and soggy, in which case who would want to? Even when an implement is obviously required (think hollandaise), asparagus can be used to shock the unwary if an asparagus holder or a pair of small tongs is used instead of a mere fork.

Bagels and lox. Bagels and lox are finger food, but the fashion now (if delicatessens can be said to indulge in fashions)

The Mannerly Person's Revenge

An advantage of knowing table manners is the ability to shock people, as the lady on the left is doing, by using esoteric etiquette. That young whippersnapper in the middle thinks that the more formal the occasion, the more silver is required, but he is wrong. While eating asparagus with a fork is allowed—as are individual asparagus tongs, for those lucky enough to have them—asparagus stalks may quite properly be eaten with the fingers. The only error here is his using a knife on a vegetable.

He has also managed to annoy the waiter by inching toward the young lady so that there is no room between them, making it awkward for the waiter to serve him, which must be done at the diner's left, or to clear the young lady's plates, which is done from the diner's right.

is to serve the parts separately and require the person who ordered it to put it together in a sandwich. Therefore, a knife is required for the cream cheese, and a fork to lift the lox and onions into place.

Bouillon. Tiny round bouillon spoons exist, but technically no utensil need be used. You can't actually scoop bouillon up in your cupped hands, but you can properly lift a two-handled bouillon cup and drink straight from it.

Breads. Bread rules depend on fiber—their fiber, in determining which you cut and which you tear, and your moral fiber, in refraining from attacking every type of bread with a knife or slathering it with butter and sweet stuff all at once.

A slice of bread, or a roll or muffin, is torn—not in half, but in one portion of two or three bites at a time. This is buttered and eaten before another such portion is torn. Croissants are also eaten this way. (Miss Manners knows this makes a mess. Would it help if she told you that croissant flakes are not socially unacceptable unless they stick to the tip of one's nose?) English muffins, being somewhat stronger, may be broken in half and made into half sandwiches. So may bagels, but being even stronger, they may be cut with a knife. When the bread is really stronger than you are—biscotti, for example—it must be weakened before it starts asking Miss Manners whether it should break your teeth in half or into smaller bits. Therefore, unlike other breads, it may properly be soaked in coffee.

Candy and nuts. Bonbon spoons may be used to convey candy from the serving dish to the hand, and nut spoons to convey nuts along the same route. If you use bare fingers, the rule, once also applied to courtship, is that the one you squeezed is yours.

Chicken. (Please see Poultry.)

Clams, mussels or oysters on the half shell. These are showered with a squeezed lemon or dabbed with sauce, and then held by that shell in one hand while the other goes after them with the small seafood fork. Lifting the shell and drinking the juice is forbidden only in the presence of real tablecloths.

Long-necked clams are grabbed by their long necks—vicious as this may sound—stripped, dunked in water to get rid of the sand (this water is called broth and may be drunk afterwards by those who enjoy drinking their dishwater), dunked in butter and put by hand into the mouth.

Traditions of daring notwithstanding, oysters have to be chewed. It is dangerous to confuse the rule that oysters are taken into the mouth whole, rather than cut on the plate, with the idea that they must continue uncut all the way down to the tummy.

In the first place, you wouldn't get any flavor out of them that way, thus making the process an expensive way to eat horseradish. In the second place, you would have to have the Heimlich maneuver performed on you and it is impolite to shoot whole oysters across the room from your throat.

Corn on the cob. Corn on the cob is easy only for those who don't care if they leave a pattern on the cob that looks like the smile of someone who has never visited a dentist. Sometimes their teeth look like that, too. Corn should be eaten in an orderly fashion; otherwise, the conversation quickly turns to its association with pigs.

Desserts. Cakes and pies require the use of a fork, and not everybody has pastry forks. The small plain fork, with or without a cutting edge (or two cutting edges, which must delight the left-handed) that appears under the name of fish, salad, tea, or youth fork is always ready to volunteer at dessert time, as which of us is not.

Gooey desserts require a spoon, and as any greedy person knows, a teaspoon is not enough. A nice big oval dessert spoon is what is needed, although there are tiny shovels for the dainty, which take only a bit of unadorned ice cream, custard or, better yet, sherbet, and long slim spoons (usually the iced tea spoons in disguise) for parfaits.

Regular ice cream forks have both bowls and tines for obvious reasons. These can operate alone. But there is no sweet dessert worth the name that wouldn't be better approached with the standard proper dessert service of both fork and spoon, so that neither a crumb nor a drop need be missed.

Dips. You only get one dip, so take as much as you can without getting it all over yourself. Seeing a cracker or carrot stick returned from the mouth to get seconds revolts everyone else at the party. (Please see Double-Dipping, page 27.)

Eggs, soft-boiled. One may use a small egg spoon (or even a demitasse spoon willing to do overtime by working the day shift), rapping smartly on the top until the shell shatters into pieces that may be picked off delicately with the fingers. There is also a special egg guillotine for the purpose, decorated with a chicken motif, a device which does not bear philosophical examination but works very well.

In any case, the small amount of white left in the top is eaten with the spoon. We do not smush and swirl (unless we are eating Fudge Whirl ice cream alone at home with the shades down). You must exert yourself to season your egg as you go. If not for choruses of "Please pass the salt," there would be no conversation at all at the civilized breakfast table.

Fast food. The typical fast food is a gnarly brownish object the size of (and often found in) a toddler's fist, known variously as chicken, clam, potato, onion or fish. It's not pretty, but it can be satisfying. However, it is served on a paper plate with a small plastic container of ketchup, tartar sauce or melted butter balanced on top of the food. The total equipment provided is a fork of white plastic as delicate as the thinnest china teacup and a napkin the size, but nowhere near the thickness, of a note-sheet. The correct way to eat it begins with putting the sauce dish to one side on the table, much as one removes a finger bowl from the dessert plate in formal service. No, wait. It begins with going back and getting six more paper napkins. It ends with ignoring the flimsy fork and picking each object up by one end, dousing it one bite at a time. All right, you would have done it that way without instruction.

Finger foods. Pretzels, popcorn, cheese snacks, deviled eggs, potato chips, cookies, candy and, for the more advanced among us, raw vegetables, canapés served on crackers or in firm little graspable shapes and celery may always be eaten by hand. Other possibilities, notably chicken, require proximity to close relatives or to trees.

Fish. Fish knives and forks, which epitomize Miss Manners' idea of the proper tool for the proper food, are nevertheless in questionable repute among crusty old-timers—even though they agree that anyone who uses a meat knife on fish will sprout tadpoles between the fingers. The old-fashioned alternative is to use two forks at once.

There are two accepted ways of avoiding the fish bones. One is to avoid putting bones in your mouth by picking them out with the sharp tip of a fish knife, if one is provided, or with the fork. The backup method is to remove fish bones from the mouth with the fingers. You are not going to believe that this is the proper method (as opposed to how one removes indigestible parts of meat or poultry—depositing them back on the fork), but Miss Manners promises you that it is.

Fondue. Fondue is cooked by the individual diner at table by the spear, dip and drip method, whether it is a chunk of bread to be coated with cheese, meat to be cooked in oil, or fruit to be slipped into bubbling chocolate. The item is secured to a long cooking fork, and then transferred to the plate by pulling it off with the regular fork, and is eaten with the latter. You are not allowed to drip on the table on the way from pot to plate, but unfortunately are going to do so anyway. Fondue hosts should not use their best tablecloths.

Frogs' legs. Technically, one may eat frogs' legs by hand, but since everyone else in the restaurant will assume that the item in hand is a particularly scrawny chicken, the fastidious do not. At any rate, they clean them up first, by separating the bones and taking off most of the meat with knife and fork.

Fruit garnishes on cocktails. Take the fruit slice in one hand, the glass in another, and take a sizable swig from the latter. Then throw the fruit into the drink where, according to Archimedes' principle, there will now be room for it to displace some liquid without its making the drink overflow.

This tends not to work after the third drink. But by then the drinker is likely to be more interested in the possibility of wearing the fruit slice as a nose decoration, anyway.

Fruits, whole. Miss Manners realizes that the frank hand-to-mouth technique of fresh juice dribbling on the chin is fun, and it is perfectly proper with fruit plucked directly from orchard or lunch box. At table, however, the trick is to eat the peach—or apple, apricot, pear or plum—without ever touching it with one's hands. One stabs it with the fruit fork and cuts the side off with the fruit knife, away from any pits; then cuts that half into quarters and eats each with the fork. If you're experienced at this, you might try peeling it in a nice long spiral; novices are advised to pretend they love the peel. (However, not all fruit peel can be eaten: The hairy hide of a kiwi would make you ill all over the tablecloth, and that does not make a favorable impression.)

Cantaloupe and other melons are eaten with a spoon when served for breakfast; at dinnertime, melon served for dessert is properly eaten with a fruit knife and fork. Those who cannot handle the ambiguity should invest in those little kitchen gadgets that turn melons into melon balls.

Cutting away the peel of melon and pineapple sections is easy—and so is watermelon, if you resist the temptation to spit the seeds across the table and merely scrape them away with the knife.

Cutting away the peel of a persimmon is difficult, even if one stands it upright, but it is possible. Cutting away the peel of an orange or tangerine without touching it—or daring it to squirt you—is well nigh impossible.

Strawberries are eaten with a strawberry fork, a cute little thing with long tines that almost nobody provides. They may be eaten hand-held by the stem if there is one, or with a spoon if there isn't.

A spoon is also used for scooping everything out of a pomegranate half (the seeds are edible), or discarding the seeds and scooping out the rest of a papaya. (Once you have mastered that, please see Mangoes.)

Fruit, cooked. Fruit that has been previously subdued through stewing or being cut into tiny bits is eaten with the standard dessert spoon and/or fork.

Garnishes. Food that appears on a plate, with the exception of those items that turn out to be painted on the china, is intended to be eaten. There is something about the idea of using perfectly good food for decoration, with the requirement that it be thrown away uneaten, that Miss Manners finds offensive.

Grapes. Grape shears enable one to do hand exercises around a grape stem before concluding that they need to be sharpened and just plucking the grapes. The correct way to get rid of grape seeds is to isolate them in the mouth with the tongue and then to deposit them quietly in one's closed fist, rather than to have the fist come in after them.

Gravies and sauces. Gravies and other sauces may properly be smeared over foods, provided the proportion of plate to sauce remains in favor of the plate. There is such a thing as a sauce spoon—nearly flat with one side higher—but usually one must reconcile oneself to not being able to get it all.

Gum. What is the proper etiquette for disposing of gum at the dinner table? Oh, just stick it onto a table leg like everyone else.

No, no, no—Miss Manners is only jesting. One cannot properly chew gum in front of other people at all, and therefore this etiquette problem does not exist. A polite person would never be anywhere near a dinner table with chewing gum.

Ice cream cones and sandwiches. In the race between greed and nature, nature usually wins by melting the ice cream faster than it can be gobbled. The polite person tends to his or her drips and potential drips before biting.

Ice cream drinks. Virtually every sweet fast food that is traditionally ordered by saying, "Oh, what the heck, I'm going to go ahead and have [a milkshake, a frappe, a crushed ice concoction, an ice cream soda]," requires a spoon.

Even if there is a straw and the stuff is not too bloated with calories to get through that straw, the spoon has two essential purposes: mushing it all up, which is prohibited by etiquette but may be politely accomplished anyway by stirring everything vigorously; and getting that last drop. Miss Manners stands by a rule she made in her comparative youth— that everyone is allowed three (but no more) noisy slurps at the end of an ice cream concoction, simply because it is a crime to let that good stuff go to waste. A more decorous way of getting the last drop is to use the straw as a pipette and allow its contents to dribble back into the spoon.

Iced tea. The earliest iced tea etiquette (iced tea was invented in the United States at the beginning of this century) suggested saucers for iced tea glasses but failed to make them mandatory, resulting in wet tablecloths. The proposed solution of making iced tea an exception to the rule against leaving spoons in drinks resulted in a number of damaged noses.

Miss Manners suggests going back to providing saucers. The polite person not given one can only prop the iced tea spoon against whatever plate is available.

Lamb chops. Lamb chops are the sissies of the otherwise big tough (in attitude only, one hopes) meat gang. Secretly they yearn to be torn off by the teeth, but they are timid about being roughly handled. So they go in for silliness, such as little paper frills, which are supposed to protect the diner's hands.

Miss Manners declares herself too shocked by the sight of lamb chops in underpants to countenance such a thing. In any but the most informal family meals, chops should not be picked up, anyway. For family meals, a more sensible fancy touch would be finger bowls or hot damp terrycloth towels.

Lasagna. Lasagna and its cheese-dripping relatives can be twirled, although cheese tends to expand to compete favorably with a hungry person's patience. For that reason, the forkful may be tilted against the plate so that it is cut by the side of the fork.

Mangoes. Mangoes not eaten in the bathtub should not be attempted with the fingers. Juice running off the nose is not a pretty sight.

The fingers should instead be gripping a fruit knife and fork, with which one quarters, pits and skins the fruit into a respectful attitude. How? By subduing it with the fork while cutting it in half with the knife and then, with the cut part against the plate, cutting away the skin with the knife while the fork holds it in place. Then remove the stone and cut the mango into quarters and eat it with the fork.

Some successful slicers have, however, objected to the idea of skinning the mango after the sides are cut. A popular alternative they cite is: "Cut two lines down the length, but NOT through the skin, then cut crosswise several times, making squares. Now turn each half inside out, making the cut squares stand out. Put them on a plate with a fruit knife and fork."

If you want to save your friends, linens and wallpaper, you should halve and pit the mango in the kitchen and serve it to them with a dessert spoon to scoop out the flesh.

Olives. If olives are wholesomely consorting with raw carrots and celery, as we all probably should be, they are eaten with the fingers. If they appear in a salad, they cannot expect special treatment—the same salad fork used for the other ingredients may pick them up at will.

If an olive is immersed in alcohol, you should (eventually) drain off the entire drink (for the olive's own good, of course) and then tilt the glass and roll it toward its fate.

As for unpitted olives or unpitted anything else, the trick is to eat around the pit—inside the mouth, with the mouth kept closed. The mouth is then opened just enough to discreetly deposit the pit into the utensil it used on the trip to the mouth, even if that utensil happens to have been the hand.

Onion rings. Fried onion rings served in a fast-food restaurant may be eaten with the fingers, as they probably couldn't be subdued with a plastic fork. Onion rings on a steak dinner in a reasonably formal restaurant are cut and then eaten with a fork.

Onion soup. French onion soup is like some romances—you know you're going to make a fool of yourself, but it's so good you don't care.

This is not to say that Miss Manners tolerates waving cheese strings about until they catch on the chandelier. The spoon is the only tool to be used, but the mess can be minimized by the twirling technique. Soggy bread does not put up much of a fight against the spoon's edge, and the cheese may be forced downward into the soup very slowly and be turned—very, very, very slowly—below sea level, so to speak.

Pasta salads. Pasta salads are, in theory, scooped up with the fork, but in fact they must be stabbed to be captured. The compromise is to stab them with the fork held tines up.

Peking duck. Peking duck is made into a nice little package with the ends tucked in and then eaten with the hands. You can argue that forks and knives are not required because they are not a Chinese tradition. Miss Manners hastens to add that they are not actually wrong in Chinese restaurants, either, especially on the part of people whose alternative is flying food.

Pizza. There are gooey pizzas and pizzas that have been baked senseless. No one should have trouble eating the latter by hand under all but formal circumstances, but the age of the eater affects the way gooey pizza is eaten. Grown-ups with strings of cheese all over their faces look a lot worse than young people in the same condition. They should therefore employ forks on which to wind any hanging parts.

Potatoes, baked. Baked potatoes confound those etiquetteers who like everything to make sense (Miss Manners, who revels in philosophic chaos, is not one of these) and claim that there is a logical reason (as opposed to tradition, which is always interesting but seldom logical) for all table manners.

One of their prime examples is the ban against using one's meat knife on fish or salad—the explanation being that meat knives have steel blades that would corrode from lemon or vinegar. Okay, but one is also banned from using one's meat or any other knife on potatoes. Why? Because so many people eat potatoes with lemon juice? One is just not supposed to, that's all; one is supposed to use one's fingers to split the potato (Yow! It's hot!) and a fork to mash in the butter or sour cream.

Poultry. We all know that plainly cooked poultry tastes better from the hands, but it is permissible to eat it that way only at picnics and very informal meals. The reason that chicken and ducks are soaked in wines and slathered with sauces when they are served at more formal dinners is to compensate for the fact that they must be eaten with knife and fork. As for very tiny game birds that look pathetic on the plate, there should be no temptation to eat them *from* the bone because one may *eat* the bones.

Salad. Once again, one should not use a knife on a salad—unless it is a salad knife, a small, straight, useful and unfortunately rare item. The equipment usually supplied is only one fork. One lettuce leaf alone requires being cut into four pieces to be eaten decently by anyone except a bunny rabbit, who does not mind letting the unnibbled portion hang out of the mouth until needed. Bunny rabbits are rarely invited out twice.

Whoever prepares the salad has a choice of providing a salad knife or cutting the salad ingredients into manageable pieces. When neither has been done, etiquette demands that the eater use the edge of the fork to rip things apart, but etiquette also secretly sympathizes with the desperation that leads to using an inappropriate knife.

The sides of salad forks, like the minds of people who serve oversized salad chunks, are not known for their sharpness. The fact that so many would-be diners give up is probably what has given rise to the defeatist notion that the lettuce was not intended to be eaten anyway. (Please also see Tomatoes.)

Sandwiches. Anyone can eat a tuna fish on rye. And anyone can eat a two-bite, triangular cucumber sandwich at a tea party, provided Miss Manners doesn't get to it first. The trick is to eat a sandwich, or variation thereof, in which the stuff inside moves and expands as you demolish the bread.

Miss Manners did not intend this to sound as if she is talking about battling an alert eel that has crawled into a baguette. What she had in mind was:

• *Club sandwiches.* There is no preventing shreds of bacon and lettuce from making a break for freedom once the toothpick is removed, as it must be if luncheon is not to be followed by surgery. Compress a quarter of the sandwich in the hand, encouraging any escapees to hit the plate, rather than the shirt front. These may be eaten with a fork after the sandwich is finished.

• *Pita.* The idea is to stuff the stuffing back in before it gets away. One should open the pocket slightly—fold down, to catch any sauce—so that fillings naturally fall back inside. A discreet poke may be forgiven.

• *Heroes.* The gripping surface is so highly developed as to make holding this easier than eating it. Discreet crushing is advised, followed by nibbling up whatever shoots out from under the bread.

• *Tacos.* The emerging insides must be rigorously pruned. A pattern of eating from the folded corner to the center allows the lower part to provide a gripping surface until the end.

• *Hot dogs.* Accepting the tragedy that you will never make the hot dog come out even with the bun saves a lot of trouble. Just don't fill out that blank end of bun with globby mustard or ketchup, much less relish, because the hot dog will kick it out the back while you're not looking.

• *Sloppy Joes, roast beef with gravy and other sandwiches in which the bread gets soaked to oblivion.* Don't be silly, use a fork. Miss Manners is sorry that she can't also provide you with a spoon, but there are limits. Who ever heard of eating a sandwich with a spoon?

Shellfish. Crab and lobster served in their shells without having been removed, mayonnaised and sneaked back in are quite properly eaten with messy gusto. And the person who knows how to do it can be spared the indignity of a bib.

Legs are pulled off and eaten by hand, claws and bodies crushed with metal crackers or wooden mallets, and the meat speared with sharp little forks. Any of this may be dipped into butter or other sauces, after which a quick flick of the wrist over the dish would be enough to protect the diner's clothes. In the soft-shell stage, the entire crab is eaten, so a fish knife is practically mandatory.

Shrimp served in its shell is picked apart with the fingers (Warning: Do not attempt with fresh manicure) and eaten by hand. When it is peeled, as when a number of them hang on the edge of a stemmed glass bowl like so many swallows on a telephone wire, shrimp is eaten with a seafood fork. When it is peeled only to near the tail, the diner has been had. There is no way of extracting any shrimp from its peel with a fork, just as there is no way to find a receptacle at a cocktail party for a frilled toothpick extracted from a shrimp.

Shish-kabob is removed from its stick by holding the stick against the plate and pulling the food off with the fork. Therefore, shish-kabob served as an hors d'oeuvre (as if one could nibble it like corn on the cob, and in a standing position at that) is a menace.

Snails. Snails served in the shell are held by special little gripping devices, while the snail is stabbed with the two-pronged snail fork and the garlic butter is dribbled on the plate, where a bread mop on a fork can be sent after it. That's the best part, anyway.

Soup. The penalty for eating one kind of soup with the equipment intended for another is not severe. Compared with the punishment for mishandling any equipment while one is eating soup—a swift punishment invoked not by etiquette so much as by gravity—it is quite mild.

Basically, soup is served in two-handled cups at luncheon and in soup plates at dinner. Hot soups are served in plates and cold ones, including jellied soups, in cups. The large oval spoon is intended for clear soups, the large round spoon for cream soups, and a smaller round spoon for broths. Only formal dinners, where there is going to be so much to eat that we can't risk filling people up with thick soups, require strict observance about clear soup in plates. For less formal dinners, and even formal dinners in summertime, the cold soup routine, complete with cups and round spoons, is permissible. If you want to serve a hot soup at lunch on a cold day—well, as Miss Manners said, the penalty is not severe.

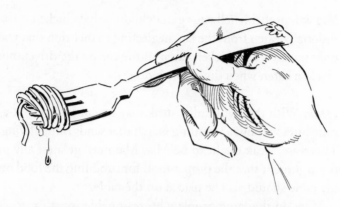

What Your Italian Grandmother Didn't Tell You

She taught you to make a proper forkful of long pasta by twirling the fork, and she may even have demonstrated by bracing the fork in the bowl of a spoon. What she forgot to mention—or did, but you forgot—is that the fork is properly twirled against the plate, not a spoon. If you had learned to eat chicken from your southern grandmother during her famous backyard barbecues, you would still be in trouble if she caught you gnawing chicken bones from your hand at her proper dinners.

Soup cannot be eaten with chopsticks. Therefore the Chinese provide a porcelain spoon for the purpose, while a Japanese lacquer soup bowl may be lifted to the mouth for direct drinking.

Spaghetti. Spaghetti is twirled on the fork against the plate until it makes a reasonably neat package that can be brought to the mouth without more than an inch overhang. Same for other long pasta, of whatever width, going under whatever name.

No, a spoon is not properly used as the twirling place for the fork, and no, not in Italy, either. Miss Manners means no disrespect to your Italian grandparents who told you it was.

You will probably tell your grandchildren that chicken is traditionally eaten from the lap, neglecting to mention that you only meant fried chicken eaten in the car by the driver, not chicken eaten when dining with others.

Steak. With the right knife, steak may be cut into one-at-a-time bites without a wrestling match that sends things flying. Therefore, steak ought to be Miss Manners' greatest ally in the argument that the proper tools for subduing the food on the table should also be placed on the table.

Why do the same people who reasonably insist on steak knives for eating steak sneer at the idea that fish knives should be provided for eating fish? (Never mind. Miss Manners doesn't want to hear what steak lovers think of people who prefer sole amandine.)

Sushi and sashimi. Sushi is lifted clear from the plate with chopsticks, delicately dipped into the soy sauce (to which some industrial-strength green horseradish has been previously added and stirred with the chopsticks) and then to the mouth, preferably to be eaten in one huge bite. This is so much fun that Miss Manners is reluctant to admit that the fingers may be used instead. This laxity does not extend to sashimi, which must be eaten with chopsticks or a fork.

Tomatoes. Miss Manners suggests that you not try to stab cherry tomatoes and eat them in bites. They have ways of getting even.

When the people who were supposed to be cutting up tomatoes before serving them let you down, you have little choice but to cut a large tomato with the side of the fork, or to put an entire cherry tomato into the mouth and clamp down on it with lips firmly shut.

Vegetables. The most staple and, one would think, trustworthy vegetables have one or another nasty little trick to play. With peas, it is Catch Me If You Can, in which the handicap is that it's no fair mashing them into insensibility. With spinach, it's I'll Get You Later. Beans' trick Miss Manners doesn't even want to mention.

Vegetables must be pursued with the unaided fork, although there is nothing to stop the wily hunter from cornering them against another item on the dish, such as a solid mound of mashed potatoes or a piece of bread that just happens to be held nonchalantly in the left hand.

Yogurt. Yogurt requires not only a spoon but also the counterintuitive knowledge that the fruit is at the bottom. Fortunately, it says so on the package. Unfortunately, Miss Manners does not allow people to eat from the package except under the very least formal of circumstances. So she requires those who serve yogurt to others to put the goodies on the top.

CHAPTER 3

BASIC EATING RITUALS

SOLITARY EATING

Technically, there are no etiquette rules in operation when one is home alone. Even the ubiquitous Miss Manners is prevented from observing what might go on in solitude behind closed doors—both by the law and by having more interesting things to do. Everyone needs an occasional bathrobe day, she recognizes, and it is best not to know what standards of civilization do or do not prevail then.

Of course, if there are violations that leave a mess for someone else to clean up, they no longer qualify as private acts. But manners are a social form and the mandate to use them should not apply when no one else is affected. Miss Manners has been known to tout this loophole as an advantage of manners over the relentless restrictions of morality. If you commit an immoral act, whether or not others are able to detect it or to punish you for it, it is still immoral. You will have to answer to your conscience and your God. But unmannerliness that is not detected doesn't count. If nobody saw it, you're off free; you don't even have to answer to Miss Manners.

However, just when she is basking in the relief that greets this soft and tolerant attitude, Miss Manners has been known to snap, "But of course, no self-respecting person would ever put the milk carton on the table, even with all the shades drawn."

Partly, she does this to protect her reputation against the charge of being sweet and reasonable. Wimpiness, along the lines of "Oh, do whatever makes you feel comfortable," is part of what was destroying the very notion of etiquette's importance before Miss Manners charged in, armor clanking, to rescue it. There is also an essential point in the milk-carton remark. (You do understand that the milk carton contains as much symbolism as milk, don't you? Good.) Without taking back the statement about etiquette's governing behavior that affects other people, Miss Manners can identify some murky areas where unobserved behavior ought nevertheless to follow some standards.

The simplest argument is that the person who behaves like a pig when alone is apt to do so before others. Indeed, it is often claimed that being with one's family or roommates is, regarding the question of etiquette, tantamount to being alone. People who declare that true intimacy means you don't have to worry about being polite will quickly run out of people who want to be intimate with them.

Even if it were possible to avoid making etiquetteless solitary behavior a habit that spills over—and onto—others, Miss Manners would still raise that question of self-respect.

Is there a standard of etiquette that you owe to yourself? She believes that there is. The person who eats as meticulously when alone as in front of others is practicing an ennobling kind of self-etiquette. Miss Manners also promises that the person who sets a nice table will be happier than the person who doesn't use a saucer under every cup and bowl. All right—who doesn't actually sit down to eat. All right—who doesn't actually use eating tools.

UBIQUITOUS EATING

Whew. What a massive effort it took to convince people of the simple notion that courtesy limits the places in which smoking is permitted—name-calling, families divided, legal threats, bodies left lying in the streets where the cigarette butts used to be.

Miss Manners doesn't think she can live through that again. Yet there is work to be done in enforcing the rule that food and drink ought not to be consumed indiscriminately, in any place, no matter what else happens to be going on. There are proper places in which to eat and drink—six on every city block, with fast-food delivery trucks running past them every minute to rescue the stranded—but classrooms, houses of worship, public transportation, sidewalks and concert halls are not among them.

One has only to point this out to raise the cry of deprivation. (Chomp, chomp, chomp.) We live in the era of the grain bag, when sustenance is carried everywhere. The alternative to the-world-as-dining-room is pictured as starvation. (Chomp, chomp, chomp.) When was the last time you heard anyone talk of skipping eating because it might spoil the appetite? During dinner, in reference to saving room for dessert, that's when.

In the matter of the modern smoking bans, Miss Manners can hardly claim an etiquette victory—if victory it can be said to be at this stage, when both sides behave equally badly. There was always, and still is, an etiquette rule against smokers smoking near non-smokers without asking their permission. There was just the small problem, for about the last three quarters of a century, that smokers refused to obey it.

So the law had to take over. Only when non-smokers ventured the argument that vicariously received smoke was actually injurious to their health were they able to enlist the law to ban smoking from public areas. So far, no one has been able to prove vicarious food poisoning. Why should anyone who feels like eating not do so on the spot, just because the noise, sight, garbage or trash may bother others?

Voluntary self-restraint for the common comfort, which is what etiquette depends on (because it lacks the authority to send people to jail), is not the rage these days. So Miss Manners has been trying to think of selfish reasons to offer people for not annoying others with their eating or showing them the disrespect of divided attention:

• People who eat all day long at their desks receive no extra credit when they eat lunch at their desks. If it were not the custom to snack while working, one could gain a reputation as a tireless worker merely by bringing in a sandwich at noontime.

• If students and workers are able to eat and drink while doing whatever they are really supposed to be doing, there is no need for the recess and the coffee break.

• The unabashed display of food and drink that people have brought for themselves increasingly appears to others to be a buffet table in which they can reasonably ask to participate. It is true that there is an etiquette violation in sniffing around other people's supplies asking plaintively, "May I have some of that?" Miss Manners wishes to point out that it is not quite nice, either, to display tempting provisions when other people don't have their own meals in front of them.

• Miss Manners has always been bewildered that people

who discover posh restaurants are in a panic about how properly to eat in them. It appears that eating eleven times a day does not prepare one for what is seen as an amazing trial—the ability to navigate one's way through an actual meal.

• Finally, eating when sitting down at a table, with all the necessary eating tools provided, saves dry cleaning bills.

Miss Manners has now succeeded in making herself feel very modern by arguing her case with appeals to such motives as impressing headwaiters and not having to share. The truth is that she believes refraining from eating and drinking—and smoking—at will should be done because controlling behavior so as not to offend others is the basic step toward civilization, and the rituals of communal eating are necessary to transmit and confirm civilized life. The rituals of eating are, as any anthropologist can attest, some of the strongest cultural bonds that a society can share.

BREAKFAST

Does etiquette have a hard time getting its act together in the morning? Miss Manners acknowledges that one might think so after surveying the lackadaisical material etiquette supplies as rules for breakfast.

At family breakfast, it permits people to arrive and depart on their own schedules, grunt rather than converse, and read at the table—as long as they are reading the newspaper rather than a cereal box or milk carton. Even at breakfast, cartons don't belong on the table. However, there are more refined ways of having breakfast.

BREAKFAST TRAYS

The proper breakfast tray features a small-scale china set with covers over the eggs and toast, not only to keep these items warm but to ease the jolt of seeing food at that hour; individual-size salt and pepper shakers, jam jar, sugar bowl and cream pitcher, so as not to overwhelm one with the strain of lifting the full-size items; a small napkin, in case the motor skills are not up to shaking out a big one; and a single flower, because the scent of a bouquet would be overpowering. This is accompanied by the newspaper (preferably ironed first), although ideally one should get a partial news summary that leaves the distressing news for later.

The only thing that seems to be missing is someone to fix the tray, carry it upstairs, gently open the curtains so as to let in a few weak rays of daylight, and collect the dirty dishes after a discreet interval.

BREAKFAST PILLS

DEAR MISS MANNERS—I visit someone occasionally at her home, and we normally sit down for breakfast. She will bring to the table a small bowl of pills that she will take. Meantime, I wonder if I should begin to eat. Is her taking of her pills tantamount to the host picking up her fork?

GENTLE READER—Well, let's see. Vitamin pills constitute nourishment, and can therefore be interpreted as beginning breakfast. Aspirin, however, may be interpreted as an antidote to previous social activities, which you may or may not wish to discuss.

But then, some people don't want to discuss anything at breakfast. So just drink your orange juice. Breakfast, Miss

Manners is pleased to be able to report, is the one meal that guests may begin before their hosts—including before their hosts are awake.

THE POWER BREAKFAST

Unlike household breakfasts, the restaurant breakfast demands absolute punctuality. So do lunch and dinner appointments, but being late to breakfast is worse because it gives the other person time to think about missed sleep.

Another rule that goes double then is the one against discussing what other people do or do not eat. Comments such as "How can you eat that much at this hour?" "Just coffee? Don't you know that breakfast is the most important meal of the day?" and "Do you know how much cholesterol you have on that plate?" are rude when uttered by anyone except one's mother, and not very pleasant then.

Business breakfasts are, by definition, brief, and the departure line is, "Well, I'm afraid I have to be getting to work." Doing telephone work at the table, making or receiving calls (other than one's child's emergency "I can't find my shoes!"), is rude.

BED AND BREAKFAST

Spontaneous houseguests must offer to hurry away after the merest suggestion of breakfast, while convincingly looking as if they wanted to stay. That way, a host or hostess who sees the expression can protest, while one who chooses not to may say good-bye.

COFFEE IN THE OFFICE

DEAR MISS MANNERS—My co-workers and I know that one should never eat from a container or carton, but what about coffee or tea? Almost everyone picks up a container of coffee every morning. Must we transfer it to a regular cup? Must we have a saucer? Are mugs acceptable?

GENTLE READER—What do you mean, "must"? If you do not, will Miss Manners come to your office every morning and knock the paper cups out of your hands?

No. Why should she? Someone, probably you, is bound to knock them over anyway, all over the work you just finished. Ask, rather, if life and coffee (many people think you really cannot have one without the other) will be more pleasant if you use cups and saucers.

Yes, indeed.

BREAKFASTS, TOO EARLY
AND TOO LATE

Midday is when etiquette begins paying attention to breakfast. Before rolling over and going back to sleep, it recommends a hearty spread for your friends who come by on Sunday in their best tweeds or exercise clothes.

"Can't you just put out some nice silver chafing dishes with eggs and kippers for the hearty?" it asks, the unspoken ending of the question being "and let me alone for just a few moments?"

"Better yet, why don't you go chase a fox around the woods for a few hours? We'll have a nice hunt breakfast when you get back, at, say, twelve or twelve-thirty." It gets positively energetic about wedding breakfasts, which take place after noon weddings, and counsels a good five courses, beginning with a delicate soup. The less said about the bride's and bridegroom's actual first breakfasts that day—such as whether the coffee prescribed to shake off the effects of the night before will encourage such jittery thoughts as "Am I throwing my life away?"—the better.

It suggests offering debutantes and those rowdy boys they found heaven-knows-where a delicately luxurious breakfast at two or three in the morning. This is a duty the rich owe the community—keeping their offspring off the streets.

LUNCHEON

The essential ingredient for a proper luncheon is time—time to prepare a meal for guests, time to go to someone's home and engage in leisurely conversation and time to feel pleasantly drowsy all afternoon from the pre-luncheon sherry and light wine or two with the meal. Everyone complains to Miss Manners about being fresh out of this ingredient. Sadly, she must turn her attention to more likely forms of modern lunch.

LUNCH IN THE OFFICE

DEAR MISS MANNERS—In our business establishment, some employees work in enclosed 10-foot-square offices, with two employees per office. Can you say, please, whether there might be an obligation on the part of one employee to consider the other when bringing redolent foods into the shared work area?

GENTLE READER—Redolent? Can Miss Manners have some?

But the etiquette angle of the odors that bother you is probably not "Yum—my mouth is watering and I wish I could have some." It is more likely to be "Oh, gross." Certainly anything intrusive in shared work space should be agreed upon by both workers, and that includes smells as well as noise, air and light. But you might keep in mind that there is a difference between food smells in the nose of the outsider and those in the mouth of the eater. A gentle word that you have been bothered—scrupulously avoiding insulting the food itself, much less the cuisine it may represent—should be sufficient.

If there is a wider problem and the office-mate does not accept the principle that shared space requires special restrictions, the employer must be petitioned for a more compatible arrangement, on the grounds that annoyance interferes with productivity.

SCHOOL LUNCHES

As long as it is understood that Miss Manners is not suspending the basic rules of correct dining on the grounds of youth and involuntary confinement, she will admit that the school lunchroom has an ambience all its own. The concepts of what is revolting and what is funny may not be as distinct there as in more refined establishments.

Civility is still required, but that is more apt to mean that food fights are banned than that soda cans are. Here are some of the fine points:

The fiction should be maintained that there is open seating. By that, Miss Manners means that "Go away, you can't sit here" is incorrect, although "Sorry, I'm saving these seats" is allowable if the "Sorry" is delivered without sarcasm. Claims that the table is reserved for a particular group must define such a group politely ("The junior varsity team" or "People who are studying for the English test together" is passable, but "People who don't dress like nerds" is not) and must be made with an apologetic expression.

That nobody wants to hear about other people's food dislikes is not as true here as it may be among grown-ups. General whining is considered as unpleasant as elsewhere, but the ability to amaze, disgust or convulse others by the description of what one has been given for lunch is more highly valued than in normal life.

Mutually agreeable trading is permissible. When Miss Manners was asked at an alumnae meeting of her college whether she had learned her manners there as an undergraduate, she replied, "Sure. Does anyone not want her butter?" and offered to hand over her dessert in exchange. It was not a skill she cared to carry out into the world.

Trading does not mean that sharing is required. The first rule at school, the one that got everyone's attention because it was accompanied by an adult demand to hand over one's treat, only meant that one could not consume extras without bringing enough for everyone. It did not apply to lunch.

Nor does it mean that coercion is allowed. "Hey, that looks good" requires no more of an acknowledgment from the person about to consume it than "It does, doesn't it?"

THE CAFETERIA LUNCH

DEAR MISS MANNERS—When friends meet for lunch at a cafeteria-style restaurant, I believe it is more comfortable for the first arrival to go through the line, be seated and wait, not eating, but perhaps sipping the beverage. The reason is that friends, catching up on old times, talk and stop in line, and it is awkward to choose and order food, garnish the food, pay and then find a seat. However, one friend seems disturbed to see me seated when she arrives. Another friend pointedly said, "I will meet you in front." My husband informed me that my practice of going through ahead was very rude. What do you think?

GENTLE READER—That you must like cold food. And that you must be awfully determined to make your own rules if you persist after offending your friends and disappointing your husband.

They are right, and Miss Manners fails to see why you think you are being considerate of the other patrons while sacrificing the feelings of your own friends. People who are meeting at a cafeteria should meet first, go through the line at the same time and eat at the same time. If they are going to be so excited upon seeing each other that they can't concentrate on the line, they should wait until this excitement dies down before entering the line. Your procedure can only make a friend feel dreadful for having arrived after you, even if she is not late, and for making you sit in apparent martyrdom in front of your untouched food.

THE BUSINESS LUNCH

Always eager for assistance in the arduous task she has set for herself (civilizing the world while reserving time to curl up by the fire after supper), Miss Manners tries not to probe for motives. If others are moved to help the noble cause by exhorting the citizenry to learn manners, for whatever reason, she is grateful.

But she can't help noticing that the reason most frequently given is bizarre. In its classic form, it was articulated by a law-school placement officer who stated that "the biggest fears" of students untutored in manners arise from "not knowing how to act in the presence of maitre d's, sommeliers and valet parkers" at expensive restaurants. Why does the restaurant myth have such a strong hold on the American imagination?

One reason, Miss Manners believes, is that we seem to be embarrassed by the idea of virtue. Nobody else thinks it worthwhile to suggest that good manners ought to be practiced for their own sake. Even pleasing your loved ones is ruled out as a motivation. Unlike headwaiters, family and friends are supposed to love watching you eat in the natural manner popularly known as "gross."

The desire to achieve status and make money is conferred with a legitimacy that pleasing others does not seem to have. All right, then. How important really are restaurant manners to achieving such a goal?

Miss Manners agrees that the ability to eat a meal without upsetting the appetites of others is a symbolically important skill. How a society chooses to eat—with chopsticks or forks, keeping forks in the left hand or switching them to the right— is arbitrary. But whether an individual member observes his or her own society's conventions is a good indication of whether that person is basically civilized, that is, knowledgeable in the ways of the society and considerate enough to practice them.

Of course, this is done for the benefit of fellow diners. A good restaurant staff is too busy to monitor the table manners of its clients and too polite to indicate whether any infractions have been observed. Nor are headwaiters generally asked to make evaluations of diners to their hosts.

Familiarity with the ways of expensive haunts is, by comparison, a negligible skill. Being able to eat exotic foods without instruction, ordering wines with discrimination, or enjoying the recognition of the staff as a regular are of business value only to those aspiring to restaurant jobs. The first two can easily be learned and the third is easily bought.

If you want to learn table manners purely for the sake of an occasional expensive business luncheon, Miss Manners does not wish to discourage you. She will try to refrain from pointing out how much more motivated you should be to please those among whom you dine regularly—family and friends. However, she cannot resist slipping in the suggestion that practicing good manners on those people, every day for two or three meals a day for your entire life, is an excellent way to be sure that you will be prepared for that crucial restaurant test.

(For instructions on how to pass that test, please check The Basic Idea, page 5, and Restaurant Dining, page 100.)

A POSTSCRIPT—THE LUNCHEON HAT

DEAR MISS MANNERS—My husband and I disagree as to whether it is improper for women to wear hats indoors, or rather to leave a hat on if eating lunch, etc. I say it is proper for women to do so. Many French paintings depict women eating with large hats on.

GENTLE READER—You do happen to be right. Ladies properly keep their hats on indoors, everywhere except in their own houses, during the daytime. Luncheons even traditionally required ladies to wear hats.

But Miss Manners is alarmed at the authority you cite. Please do not—repeat, not—take your standards of decorum from what you see going on in French paintings.

AFTERNOON TEA

The chief rule, more important than not pouring hot water all over yourself and your guests, is to stop calling it "high tea." Ever alert to opportunities for gussying up the ordinary in order to make it seem expensive and chic (two concepts that are less related than many people seem to think), both dispensers and consumers of tea often mistakenly tack the word "high" onto what should be called simply "tea" or "afternoon tea."

High tea, which is held later than plain tea and has heavier food because it serves as a substitute supper, is lower in status. Miss Manners is sorry about the difficulty of mastering something so counter-intuitive, but she didn't invent this language. It comes to us from the folks who drive on the left-hand side of the road.

If you want to talk about "low" in the sense of being a dirty trick, Miss Manners suggests you apply it to the practice of providing tea-drinkers with both a nice white tablecloth and a treacherous old tea bag at the same time. Tea bags may be all very well for Formica counters, but in more genteel circumstances they are an invitation to disaster. There is nowhere to put the nasty old soggy thing, once it is removed from the teapot, except a saucer or ashtray on the way to which it will leave a telltale nasty trail.

People who serve proper tea should provide a teapot with loose tea in it, a strainer, and an extra pot of hot water. The tea pourer or drinker puts the strainer over his cup, pours tea and then adds as much hot water as necessary to get the desired strength. In practical terms, this means that the first cup is probably poured straight from the teapot, with hot water added as the pot of tea becomes, through the laws of physics, stronger and colder. There should be an extra pot of hot water, as a way of keeping things going. And a really proper tea set includes a slops bowl (Miss Manners loves the term) into which tepid dregs may be poured from one's cup before one replenishes it with hot tea. Unlike the tea bag, the strainer comes with a parking place. If the catch-the-drips bottom is attached, it swings easily aside during the straining.

Tea is properly taken straight, or with sugar, or with lemon or milk. Not lemon *and* milk, unless you want to see some disgusting chemistry, and not cream. You may have heard about putting in the milk before pouring the tea, but don't. Miss Manners offers this advice for the practical reason of being able to judge the strength of the tea by its color, rather than some nasty and complicated snobbery you don't even want to hear about. (All right: Some people's idea of a major insult is to refer to others as milk-first types.)

There are three types of finger food to be eaten with tea, and the chief thing to know is that they should be eaten in order, even though they are usually all put out at once. No fair grabbing the cookies and cake before you have had some (first course) warm bread and (second course) sandwiches. Sweets at the end, just as at mealtime. For those who can't wait, the crumpets and other hot breads may be eaten with jam or honey. Scones are laden first with jam and then with clotted cream, never the other way around. Naturally all these

Not for Sissies

Modern little girls practice giving tea parties because they plan to grow up to make profitable deals at power teas, at the expense of those who (like the little boy here who isn't paying attention) are distracted by worry about how to use all that equipment.

The two teapots may have originally been intended for India and China tea, but unless there is another pot for hot water, the larger pot would now contain water to dilute the tea to individual taste, while the smaller would contain startlingly strong tea. The traditional choice of additions—lemon, with its lemon fork; sugar, in lumps, not grains; and milk, not cream—is offered by the presiding lady. When asked for a refill, she pours the dregs from the guest's cup into that third small bowl, delicately known as the slops pot or waste bowl.

Tea food should be eaten in three stages—hot breads first, then sandwiches, then cake—but it is not always easy to keep the guests, especially escapees from other literature, from going straight to the sweets.

A proper child should also learn that this is called afternoon tea—as is the more elaborate adult version, a highly formal (and incidentally extremely inexpensive) way of entertaining—and not high tea, which is what the children get as an excuse for supper when their parents are going out.

breads are broken into two-bite-size pieces before being spread, much less consumed.

It's not really so snobbish. Tea is, after all, quieter, less complicated, cheaper, less caloric and less intoxicating than lunch. And crumbs are not held against you.

LEMON

DEAR MISS MANNERS—When I am serving tea, how should I serve the lemon? Should it be sliced or cut in wedges? Should it be put directly in the cup or handed to the guest on the edge of the saucer? If the former, do I squeeze it or just put it in? Does the guest squeeze it or put it in? Are the lemon slice and cloves removed before drinking?

GENTLE READER—Miss Manners has nothing personal against lemon wedges, but they are really not up to going out to tea. They are better off hanging out with fish, who are more their sort.

Tea is served with thin lemon slices, which sink gracefully to the bottom of the cup without making much of an impression. But then tea is so heavy with ceremony one is not supposed to mind.

Part of the ceremony is its gracious preparation by the hostess. Ladies who wouldn't have been able to find their own kitchens have prided themselves on how well they prepared tea from the leaf, using the various pots and instruments brought to them by their butlers. This includes proportioning the tea to the strength preferred by each guest and adding whatever each wants—sugar, milk or lemon. But it draws the line at squeezing someone else's lemon.

Lemon slices should be placed on a dish near the other tea

things. The hostess or the tea drinker can then put a slice directly into the cup, preferably using a dear little lemon fork with splayed tines.

Lemons stuck with cloves should be hung on Christmas trees.

TEA SANDWICHES

DEAR MISS MANNERS—At an afternoon tea in a nice hotel, I noticed other women wearing gloves and eating tea sandwiches with a knife and fork. Should I also have been using knife and fork, even though I was not wearing gloves? I had thought tea sandwiches were finger food, but I would like to know for the next time.

GENTLE READER—Next time? Do you really want a next time with that crowd?

Perhaps Miss Manners should be more sympathetic because these ladies were trying to be genteel. But etiquette considers it far worse to err on the side of pretentiousness than on that of simplicity. Tea sandwiches should be eaten with the fingers. But nothing—nothing, nothing, nothing—should ever be eaten, by any means, on any occasion, by someone who is wearing gloves.

PICNICS

As a glance through a stadium parking lot or manure-strewn field will soon make clear, there are two schools of thought about the etiquette of tailgate picnics. One of them acknowledges that standing in the wind and cold, on pavement or lumpy ground, eating from the back of a car, is a primitive form of dining. No attempt is made to do anything but pass out sustenance in the easiest fashion possible, and the license of the occasion is used to excuse serving food in plastic wrappers and cans. The other approach seeks to rise above these circumstances. Miss Manners has seen white tablecloths and floral centerpieces produced from station wagons, tailgates made into charming buffet tables, and guests issued china and silver with which to eat full meals.

Although, as might be expected, Miss Manners prefers the latter form, she does not claim that elaborate service is required for tailgate dining. As with summer picnicking, clambakes and backyard barbecues, one can consider eating outdoors to be either a welcome release from the restraints of proper indoor eating or a challenge to impose the charms of civilization on a natural setting.

Fast-food, no-frills dining is certainly a practical way of dealing with the appetite outdoors. Miss Manners tries very hard to believe that the people who are eating that way are bowing to the difficulty of the circumstances and not doing so because that's the way they eat at home as well. It couldn't be much fun to toss the rules merrily aside if you've never followed them anyway, or even known what they were. Sports fans should be the first to acknowledge the importance of observing rules and procedure to the pleasure of organized recreation.

At any rate, the people who give elaborate picnics do seem to be having more fun. There's nothing quite so smug and happy looking as someone lounging indolently on a folding chair at a charming little table, in the middle of a parking lot or field, who is peering over a long-stemmed wine glass at people eating out of paper wrappings and drinking from bottles. The same person wouldn't nearly as much enjoy eating the same meal at an outdoor restaurant where there is no shock value in the setup and everybody else is being identically and professionally served.

With either style of picnicking, there are basic amenities to be observed:

Guests must be issued the proper equipment with which to eat the food they are given. This gets Miss Manners around the necessity of tolerating paper napkins and plastic forks. In theory, these should be allowable at utilitarian picnics, but she can still bar them on the grounds that they do not give picnickers a fighting chance at their food.

At events where people are likely to know other groups present, there should be more food and drink available than necessary for the number of expected guests. Small picnic groups do not have to share with those having picnics nearby, making this one of the few situations where one is actually allowed to enjoy the contrast of the superiority of one's own dinner with that of one's neighbors. Acquaintances who stop by, trying to make conversation with watering mouths, need not be asked for the full meal, but it is customary to offer a drink and small snack to people one knows who seem to be hanging around for more than a greeting.

Other decencies must be strictly observed. Setting up a grill so as to choke other picnickers with smoke, or strewing trash around, is not allowed. It seems to Miss Manners that showing off with one's food and service is quite enough naughty fun for one afternoon without one's having to resort to the cruder methods of annoying one's neighbors.

DINNER

Etiquetteers once considered it their duty to reassure their presumably timid constituents that it was perfectly possible to serve a civilized dinner for as many as six people with the assistance of only one servant. Elaborate menus should not be attempted, hosts were warned, nor temperamental dishes. Only one soup might be offered, instead of a choice between thick and clear. Patience and indulgence would be required from the guests, who might have to push in one another's, or even their own, chairs. The simple warmth of the hosts and the rather jolly picnicky atmosphere would make up for the lack of amenities, it was explained with stunning condescension.

In that same irritating spirit, Miss Manners would like to explain that it is perfectly possible nowadays to serve a civilized family dinner without—never mind multiple servants—the services of a family member who has nothing better to do all day.

Family dinner being the cornerstone of family life, and indeed of civilization itself, the attempt must be made. By way of reassurance to those who think it beyond them, Miss Manners would like to deal with the questions (or rather, barely disguised excuses) they may not be asking but are certainly thinking.

Q: *Who is in the family, anyway? It's so hard to tell nowadays.*
A: For the purposes of family dinner, we shall define family as everyone who regularly lives in the house, whether or not those not in love with any particular one of them think so.
Q: *What time should family dinner be served?*
A: When everybody can be home, even if that means the half-hour after the children come home from school and before a parent leaves for the night shift.

Q: *Family dinner is a great idea, but it doesn't mean that I actually have to be physically present every night, does it?*

A: Yes, it does. Spiritual attendance is not taken.

Q: *What about my aerobics class?*

A: Miss Manners' admiration for your devotion to bodily fitness is exceeded only by your own, but family dinner nevertheless takes precedence.

Q: *What are we supposed to eat?*

A: You decide. This is not a nutrition guide. Anyway, Miss Manners suspects this is a trick question, designed to show that people of different eating habits cannot eat together. They can. What they cannot do is argue the virtues of their own diets over someone else's in place of conversation.

Q: *Conversation? Isn't it rude to talk while others are trying to watch their favorite programs?*

A: Yes, and for that reason no entertainment is allowed at the dinner table other than talk.

Q: *None?*

A: That's right, so stop making those noises. They're not funny.

Q: *Now wait a moment. You're not going to start in with the table manners, are you? After all, this is family. Isn't it one of the pleasures of family life that you don't have to be on your good behavior?*

A: No, that is the great pleasure, perhaps the only one, of being a hermit. The pleasure of family life comes from knowing that there are people in the world who have your own happiness at heart and are even willing to avoid forcing you to watch them chewing open-mouthed.

THE NIGHTLY RITUAL

Family dinner is a quaint old routine by which everybody in the same household would gather nightly at a specific time, rather than each head for the microwave when hungry; sit around a table, rather than stand in front of an open refrigerator; share the same food, rather than argue for competing standards of nutrition, taste and morality; and be entertained by one another's conversation, rather than by that of celebrities on television. Without in the least minimizing the demands of work, homework and working out, Miss Manners nevertheless argues that the chief ritual that binds family and civilization is sacrificed at too great a personal and social cost.

In family-style eating, platters of food are placed on the table and either passed around or served by a parent to each person in turn. The details—adults presiding and outranking children, everybody waiting until all have been served before beginning and no one leaving the table until all have finished—quietly teach the habit of respect and consideration. The requirement to take a reasonable portion—delivering it to the plate, not the mouth, and with the serving utensils, not the individual ones that also visit the mouth—reinforces the idea that nobody's appetite should ruin anybody else's.

The habit of family conversation has deeper meaning, too, which is why electronic distractions are banned. The requirement that everyone at least feign interest in everybody else's contribution not only develops social charm and disseminates family news but conveys the psychologically priceless idea that each person's daily life is important to the others.

There are parents who laboriously teach their children

The Foundation of Civilization

That may not be what family dinner looks like, especially in the immediate vicinity of the children, but that is what it is. This is because mastering table manners and other unnatural acts, such as pretending to be interested in what other people are saying while awaiting the chance to talk about oneself, require nightly practice.

Neglected children grow up with the mistaken notions that napkins are made out of paper, that napkin rings are dinner party decorations, and that teaspoons don't have to confine themselves to stirring tea but may muscle their way into place settings and falsely pass themselves off as dessert spoons.

that good manners are for public and company use only and
that rudeness is the proper expression of intimacy. Those who
give their children instruction, or send them where they may
get it in the flashy subdivisions of etiquette that require
money, but not the basics, teach them snobbery, which is bad
manners.

The most foolish of all are the parents who teach their children, through example, that spotting manners violations,
especially small, technical ones, in others gives one a right to
humiliate them. Manners should be taught firmly but kindly
to one's own children and not at all to others, because criti-
cizing others is, in itself, a rudeness.

Etiquette training for children should be slipped in casually: "Darling, please wait till you've swallowed that before you tell us about soccer practice," "No, I'm afraid
nobody wants to see how high you can build your mashed
potatoes," "Okay, everybody, please sit up and stop hunch-
ing over your plates." Notice the low-keyed tone. People
who bark etiquette orders, fail to distinguish between the
honest accident and the deliberate infraction, and issue
harsh and humiliating personal judgments do Miss Manners' cause no favor. On the contrary, unpleasant memories
of etiquette's being used illegitimately as a weapon have
probably contributed to the unfortunate downfall of the
communal meal.

Never correct a child in words when you are with guests.
It is embarrassing for the child as well as for the observers, who
may try to relieve the child's presumed feelings by chiming in
to support one or the other of you. Miss Manners does not
need to belabor the danger of seeming to criticize their behavior as well.

Lest you protest that she is betraying your noble dedication to the task of teaching your child better manners than the general standard he is likely to see, notice that she said "in words." By all means glare at your child with the classic maternal look that says, "Stop that, or I'll get you later." If you are sitting next to him, you can also jab his elbow until he finds it less painful to put it where it belongs.

SYNCHRONIZING DINNER

DEAR MISS MANNERS—My son insists that we should wait to begin until all family members are present—even if it means a wait of three or four hours. My daughter believes that unless the tardy relative has communicated a legitimate reason for the tardiness, that person should not be allowed to hold the others hostage and we should eat on schedule. Until this has been resolved, there may be no more family dinners at my house.

GENTLE READER—Miss Manners believes that dinner together every night cements family life and, indeed, civilization itself. But people who have sat around unfed for three or four hours are not going to be in any mood for civilization.

Miss Manners is pleased to see that both your son and your daughter base their arguments on respect for the occasion, but this respect must be safeguarded by stricter rules than your family seems to follow. Family dinner has to be viewed as an important engagement, not to be missed without a pressing reason. Anyone unable to be present at the time set must notify the others in advance—preferably by that morning, so that plans may be modified, but in case of a last-minute emergency, as soon as he or she knows.

That way, if anyone simply fails to show up, the other members of the family will know that it is time to panic, on the grounds that nothing except a disaster would have prevented the absent person from sending his or her extreme regrets and apologies.

CHILDREN'S FOOD FUSSING

DEAR MISS MANNERS—When our children dislike the food at mealtimes (which seems to occur on the nights they do not choose the meal), what should we do? If we insist they eat what is served, they put up a terrible fuss and beg for a sandwich instead. We want to expose them to a variety of foods so they are able to eat foods served at others' homes. Yet they seem to like so few foods. We do not want to prepare separate meals for everyone's tastes. We are in a Cuisine Quandary.

GENTLE READER—Have you not heard of such traditional parental directives as "Just have a taste, dear; you don't have to eat the whole thing, but you must taste it," and "I'm sorry, but that's what's for dinner, and we're not taking special orders," and "You don't have to like it; just eat it and say no more about it"?

Food fussery having been a staple of childish behavior since the world began, these infuriating replies were developed to save the olive and turnip markets. Eventually, they work. In, say, 15 or 20 years.

ASKING TO BE EXCUSED

DEAR MISS MANNERS—Is it rude to ask to be excused after a meal? I heard a woman tell her stepson to sit back down until everyone had finished eating, even though he had asked to be excused.

GENTLE READER—Is the young gentleman under the impression that one is at the dinner table merely to consume one's food, rather than to participate in a ritual with other people? Or that anything is allowable if one makes an excuse? If so, Miss Manners hopes he is grateful for a stepmother who teaches him otherwise.

HOLIDAY DINNERS

There are now only three American national holidays, as far as Miss Manners can observe: the Academy Awards, the Super Bowl and the Miss America Pageant. Each has its own ritual, known, understood, respected and beloved by all who participate. Lesser occasions—the modern wedding springs to mind—have been transformed by them.

What about the holidays we used to have? Thanksgiving, Christmas and the Fourth of July, for example. Anachronistically, these are still days off, and one has to do something with them until such time as they are made over into adjustable occasions on which sales are held.

Also, vestigial expectations remain about celebrating them. Miss Manners is always receiving grumbles from those who believe it is unreasonable of people to issue holiday dinner invitations on the flimsy grounds of being their relatives, although they may generously, if unhappily, agree to accept. But what are they supposed to do when they get there?

In the absence of a continued tradition, people tend to fall back on the staples, which are, in the current order of importance, Food Fussing, Asking Nosy Questions and Whining. That is everyday behavior. Miss Manners doesn't care for it then, but she would like specifically to outlaw the following holiday pastimes:

1. Any talk about food or drink other than "Do you prefer light meat or dark?" "My, this is delicious," and "Please pass the sweet potatoes" is banned from the table. Even "I'm so stuffed I think I'm going to be sick" does not come out to be the charming compliment intended.

2. Polite inquiries being not only allowable but required, it should be noted that this does not include questions about matters in which good news is announced without need of prompting. Such as "So, did you find a job yet?" and "Isn't it about time you got married?"

3. Declarations beginning with "How come I never . . ." or "How come I always have to . . ." are forbidden. And so is the tone in which they are said.

Realizing that she would thus deprive most families of all known holiday behavior, Miss Manners has two suggestions for replacement activities. If you don't mind, she will start with the second. It is just as sanctimonious as the first, but in a more generally acceptable way.

That is to open the meal itself (after there has been time for greetings and chitchat) with a discussion of the holiday being celebrated. At Thanksgiving, each person could be asked to name something for which he or she is thankful—jokes allowed, but real items also required. Someone could be asked to explain briefly the history of religious and patriotic holidays and someone else the meaning, or each person to be prepared to bring in a tidbit of information. The idea is not to have show-off time, but to start a conversation—and a family tradition, if there was not one there before.

The first idea (remember, that was the second) is to make a ceremony of the meal itself, if the particular holiday doesn't already provide a mealtime ritual. This would be no more than a family-style formal meal, which is why Miss Manners was timid about sneaking it in. It consists of a properly set table, complete with linens, centerpiece and other festive touches, but free of commercial containers; a seating and serving plan that recognizes age and station; service at the table, with a seated parent serving everyone or dishes being passed; and the rules that everyone waits to start eating until everyone is served and no one leaves the table until the meal is over.

You may recognize this as the way Miss Manners believes you should eat every evening. She anticipates the excuses that will be offered in the indignant tone of the overburdened: the whole thing is too much work, people's schedules require them to arrive late or leave early, the children get restless at a long dinner, and so on.

Too bad. This is all the more reason to make holidays sacred, so to speak, and the opportunity to make up for all those civilizing factors you told Miss Manners you didn't ordinarily have time to do. You can cut corners behind the scenes—Miss Manners is not going to check to see whether you baked those pies yourself—but not the service.

The idea is for everyone to enjoy, and for the children to learn, the deep satisfaction that a modest ritual provides. From there it is a small step toward realizing that a similarly pleasant daily routine may be worth the momentary sacrifice of such traditional rituals as watching television or dishing out unsolicited advice.

CAN FAMILY PARTIES BE AVOIDED?

DEAR MISS MANNERS—I receive invitations to holiday family parties where I feel the gathering emphasizes a great show of material things—lavishly decorated house, elaborate food, expensive gifts. The loving spirit of care isn't there. I am not impressed by the opulence.

My work is with foreign students, many living frugally. I admire their sincere work and modest lives far more than lavish displays of luxury. I would prefer to spend the holidays in simple celebrations, perhaps at a student party or visiting sick children in a hospital where caring is appreciated.

What do you think about avoiding lavish celebrations? How can one politely decline an invitation from family without hurting feelings? I feel bad about saying no, but if I go, I feel out of place and uncomfortable. Somewhere good manners must include honesty with oneself—not putting oneself in a social situation where one feels uncomfortable and must pretend.

GENTLE READER—Lots of people want to avoid going to family holiday parties, preferring to spend the time with associates of their own choice, but Miss Manners gathers that you want to receive credit for this as a virtue.

Sorry. Family duty is not something that applies only when the family is congenial or needy. And there is nothing to prevent you from both attending their events and visiting sick children.

Your relatives are your relatives and Miss Manners is sorry that their style is not your style, but that is a common family complaint. She is even sorrier that you find them cold, but she cannot urge you to be even colder by snubbing them. By your own account, their feelings for you are strong enough to make you believe that your absence would hurt them.

SYMBOLIC SHARING

DEAR MISS MANNERS—My niece is serving turkey and all the extras at Thanksgiving, but my friend never eats fowl. I thought of taking along some ham for him to eat at the dinner, but my sister said that if he doesn't eat fowl, he should decline the invitation.

GENTLE READER—Miss Manners is having some trouble with your family's interpretation of Thanksgiving. The symbolic sharing of food is off, right? The point now is for everyone to eat his or her food of choice, even if it means avoiding the communal gathering.

No, it is not. The point is still to gather and partake of what is offered, in a general, symbolic way. That does not require gobbling everything, but neither does it mean bringing one's own hoard. Your friend should have his ham before, if he wishes, and graciously accept whatever stuffing or vegetables he likes.

THE CHILDREN'S TABLE

DEAR MISS MANNERS—My grandparents' solution to having 16 relatives from around the country at a holiday dinner is to let the "children" sit by themselves at another table. Being the polite, mature young lady that I am, I have responded with the utmost graciousness. Inside, though, I am very much disturbed. I am 15 years old and I do not believe it is fair to have my age count against me in this way. Is it right to automatically consider that anyone under the age of 18 be excluded?

GENTLE READER—Excluded? You're not being excluded! You're sitting with all the great people while the grown-ups are being excluded on the mere basis of old age.

Miss Manners does not really expect you to see this at the moment. You are exactly at the time of life when it is embarrassing to be classified as a child and she is pleased that you are able to be so gracious about it. Your relatives who are younger than you are probably thrilled to be at the table with you, while those who are just a few years older are probably grateful to be where they can have sensible conversation with one another rather than entertain such questions as "What are you going to do when you graduate?" and "Do you have a girlfriend yet?"

The children's table is one of those corny family traditions that people come to value most in retrospect. In a family of Miss Manners' close acquaintance where the children are now in their twenties, the proposal to intersperse the cousins with their parents' generation was met with dismay. They had come to love being at the children's table and introducing their suitors and spouses to it.

Nevertheless, Miss Manners can get you to the grown-ups' table if you really want that. Just don't claim it on the grounds that you are big now, which will bring on a lot of silly old-people jokes. Say, "Grandma, I feel I don't see enough of you and the aunts and uncles at these parties. If you could find a place to slip me in, I'd love to get a chance to talk to you during dinner."

RESTAURANT DINING

WAITERS AND SERVICE

As an antidote to the widespread fear of sneering waiters, there should be some relief in knowing that restaurant tables are inevitably set wrong, even at the most careful places, because the setters cannot know in advance what the diners will be eating. That's why restaurants serve salad before main courses, unlike the usual practice in private houses, where there is no need to stave off starvation because dinner is already cooked.

There are only two simple things one needs to manage any restaurant meal correctly. One is the knowledge that big utensils are used for main courses and small ones for small courses; and the other is the courage to summon a waiter and say, "I don't believe I have a fork for this," even if the reason is that you dropped it on the floor.

THE PROFFERED CHAIR

DEAR MISS MANNERS—A male friend and I went to dinner at an upscale Italian restaurant, where a hostess showed us to our table and pulled out a chair, which I automatically assumed was for me.

Should my friend have taken the proffered chair and then pulled out another for me? Does a real lady only accept a chair that is offered by her male companion, or, in this day and age, is that considered passé? I believe that the lady normally takes the proffered chair, no matter the gender of the person pulling it out.

GENTLE READER—A real lady, Miss Manners feels obliged to point out, does not dwell on the gender of people who are acting in a professional capacity. And that goes double for a real gentleman.

In this day and age, and in every preceding one, up or down the scale, a real lady who sees someone holding out a chair for her has the courtesy to sit herself down in it.

ORDERING FOR OTHERS

DEAR MISS MANNERS—My wife says that the man should order all food for his party in a restaurant. That sounds very awkward to me. Can you explain?

GENTLE READER—It is awkward now, because both patrons and restaurant staff have forgotten how to do it. Most waiters seem to worry that a gentleman who says "Madam will have the pheasant" may be unauthorized to represent her and that there will be a terrible fuss and perhaps a lawsuit unless she confirms the order.

This has discouraged gentlemen from performing what was once considered a polite ritual of assuming the role of host. Miss Manners prefers that one person collect and give the orders, rather than have a crossfire of orders announced as people change their minds ("No, no, that sounds good, give me that instead"). She does not carry this preference to the point of making a greater fuss by insisting on it with a waiter who uses the 'round-the-clock method.

ORDERING EXPENSIVE ITEMS
FROM THE MENU

DEAR MISS MANNERS—One of the guests I was entertaining at a rather nice restaurant said to his wife, "The host (giving my name) has lots of money, so let's order the best on the menu." This they did, plus ordering extra drinks and an extra salad. My other guests ordered average-priced dinners. Was the first guest out of line in doing this? They are still good friends of mine.

GENTLE READER—As this bit of cuteness subjected you to both insult and injury, Miss Manners cannot imagine that you entertain a serious doubt about whether it was out of line. She can't imagine why you would continue to entertain such people, either. The rule is that a restaurant guest always orders from the middle of the menu—not the cheapest item, unless it is irresistible, and not the most expensive, unless the host announces, "You must have the lobster—it's fabulous" and orders it for himself.

Friends are certainly not supposed to mention the financial circumstances of their hosts, much less to exploit them. Perhaps you should take these friends aside and say sympathetically, with a limited offer of help, "I had no idea things were so bad that you have trouble getting enough to eat."

FOREIGN LANGUAGE MENUS

DEAR MISS MANNERS—At a lunch with my fiancée, her parents and a close friend, the menu was in Italian, which I don't speak, but they all do. As you may imagine, I had trouble ordering. I managed the main course, but then I was expected to order a salad. Unable to read the menu, I said I would share my fiancée's salad.

Fortunately, the waiter sensed my discomfort and took it upon himself to bring me a simple salad, rather than embarrassing me any further by forcing me to share with my fiancée. How can such a situation be avoided in the future?

GENTLE READER—You could try talking them all into Chinese food next time. But surely they are as likely as Miss Manners to wonder why, if you are marrying into an Italian-speaking, Italian-eating family, you are not attempting to learn at least restaurant Italian.

In the meantime it seems to Miss Manners that you have at least two people present who would be happy to assist you: the waiter, whose business it is to help people get food that they will enjoy, and your very own fiancée, whose business it has now become to help you enjoy life, as you should be doing for her. Your entire prospective family would probably have been only too glad to translate and explain the menu.

The only etiquette problem Miss Manners can imagine here is caused by your erroneous belief that it is wrong to ask for such instruction. On the contrary, it is charming. Unless you have passed yourself off as what we used to call A Count from Torcello (there are no real counts from the Venetian island of Torcello), your interest will more than make up for your ignorance.

BUFFET AND SALAD BARS

DEAR MISS MANNERS—It is my understanding that the main reason for serving meals buffet-style is to serve large groups of people more efficiently. Also, you can serve more than one entrée and a bigger variety of foods than you might at a sit-down dinner. I have always thought that the guest was to put together a proper meal on his plate and not necessarily take portions of everything on the table. You are not expected to take all the entrées, although this is not completely out of line if small portions are taken. But I have observed people making pigs of themselves, piling their plates high with food enough to feed several people. Many times, they don't even eat it all and it's wasted.

This is also true of the salad bars that many restaurants have. People come away with food piled high, thinking they have to have something of everything on the table instead of putting together a reasonably proportioned salad in keeping with the rest of the meal.

Also, many people don't seem to know the difference

between buffet-style serving and a smorgasbord. At a true smorgasbord, I believe it is permissible to approach the table three times: first for the fishes, cheeses and hors d'oeuvre–type things; second, for the cooked foods; and lastly for the desserts. Here again, it is not absolutely necessary that you take everything on the table.

GENTLE READER—Oh, boy, free food! Let's stock up while we can.

Miss Manners has also observed this approach to the open table, as restaurant patrons gleefully calculate getting one more lettuce leaf or bacon bit onto a toppling structure without having to pay extra for it. What the rationale is for buffet dinners at the homes of friends, she prefers not to think. It is, as you point out, unseemly. A truly starving but polite person would take a modest amount, eat it, drift casually back to the buffet table to take another modest amount and repeat the process until satisfied.

SLOW SERVICE

DEAR MISS MANNERS—At big benefit dinners, with 10 people at each table, should you wait to start eating after everyone has been served each course, or just the first course? Sometimes it takes a while.

GENTLE READER—Here's the procedure. Miss Manners has to warn you that it also takes a while, but once your tablemates catch on, you will have a fighting chance of eating hot food warm and cold desserts before they melt over the edge of the plate.

The first course is usually on the table or slapped down pretty quickly and so everybody waits to begin until all are served. Then comes the main course, which takes forever. Those who are served first keep their hands in their laps and bland smiles on their faces, while others are trying to signal waiters that they have been overlooked, they have ordered the vegetable platter and so on.

At this point, someone with a plate should ask, in a concerned voice, "Aren't you having dinner?" This calls attention to those who are heroically refraining from eating the dinners in front of them. The response should be something like "The service here is terrible—you go ahead and start," or "No, no, go ahead, I asked for fish." If it isn't made, those with food can resort to asking timidly, "Should we just go ahead, then?"

Nobody ever replies, "Well, no, you can just jolly well sit there until we make sure we get some food, too, because otherwise we're going to take our share of yours." Thus, manners are served, if nothing else.

TABLE TRASH

DEAR MISS MANNERS—What is one supposed to do with the foil that restaurants leave on the potato? Eat around it? Or just throw it away?

GENTLE READER—Food is not supposed to be served wrapped in storage materials, so there is no trash receptacle on a proper table (as unfortunately appear on cheap European hotel breakfast tables), because there shouldn't be any trash. Condiments, crackers, cream, non-cream, or other items that come in paper, plastic or foil should merely be opened and the crumpled trash deposited as neatly and as much out of the way as possible.

CRITTERS

DEAR MISS MANNERS—This charming city is a haven for cockroaches. I have rid my home of these pests by turning it into a wasteland of toxic chemicals. However, others have not been so successful.

Is it proper to kill one that runs across your restaurant table? What if it runs across your leg? How should one inform the staff of the restaurant? What actions or statements should one expect from the staff?

GENTLE READER—The proper statement from the staff is "How terrible! Why, this has never happened before in the history of this restaurant!" The proper action is to refuse to allow you to pay the bill, which inhibits most people from reporting the incident to the health department.

Miss Manners is afraid that to encourage this little scenario, you must seem actively repulsed by the cockroach, whether or not you murder it. Save your tolerance for your friends' roach-infested houses.

SHARING

DEAR MISS MANNERS—My female companion and I enjoy eating out, but the portion she is served is always a bit more than she can consume. She knows full well that I can finish any food that is left on her plate. What is the proper way for her to share food with me?

GENTLE READER—What stage of courtship are you in?

Miss Manners doesn't mean to be nosy—on the contrary. Etiquette demurely looks the other way when people in love enjoy offering or accepting a bite offered across the table on a fork. Normally, however, extra food is put on the bread plate and passed to the person who wants to taste or finish it.

NOT SHARING

DEAR MISS MANNERS—For 15 years I have had the pleasure of an occasional luncheon or dinner with a lovely lady friend. At just about every one of these delightful events, she has found it necessary to suggest that I try to taste a forkful of something she has on her plate.

Sometimes she hints that she would like to try something from my plate. Our food tastes are quite different, so we rarely order the same things. All her manners are especially good, with the exception of this food-tasting penchant. I consider a person's plate of food to be a very personal and private domain. My repeated suggestions that she discontinue her— in my opinion—ill-mannered table behavior prompted her to suggest that I write for your advice.

GENTLE READER—Plates can be shared only by consenting adults, and it seems to Miss Manners that you have not consented. Therefore, the lady is wrong. But since she is also lovely and otherwise well mannered, Miss Manners suggests that you ask the waiter to put a taste from your plate on a small plate for her before the food is brought to the table. If she persists with her offerings after you decline, suggest that she put them on your bread plate and then neglect to taste them.

TIMING

DEAR MISS MANNERS—My gentleman friend and I both enjoy our food when dining in restaurants but he, being much bigger than I am, enjoys more food. The result is that I am usually finished with my filet mignon and baked potato when he is still only halfway done with his king's cut prime rib (to be followed by turtle pie or some other elaborate dessert).

I already eat as slowly as I can without looking like an affected ninnyhammer, so my alternatives seem to be to stare at him as he eats, or to eat more food myself, though I am already full. Can you suggest some polite activity in which I can engage myself while waiting for my dinner partner to catch up?

GENTLE READER—Why are you dining with this gentleman if you have nothing to say to him? And why is anyone who would use such a wonderful word as "ninnyhammer" not seizing every opportunity to babble (uninterrupted, Miss Manners notes, as the gentleman's mouth would be firmly sealed around his portion of turtle pie)? Conversation is the chief reason that polite people dine in company, nourishment running only a distant, although perhaps intensely satisfying, second.

EXTRA ASSISTANCE

DEAR MISS MANNERS—A male friend says it is proper etiquette when he is on a date for him to butter his date's bread. I say he should just pass the bread. I get a free dinner if he's wrong.

GENTLE READER—You get a free dinner, but it will hardly be worth all the work you will have to do. You will have to butter your own bread, and cut up your own meat, and wipe your own little rosebud mouth afterward with your very own napkin.

Miss Manners does not argue against the performance of small courtesies by saying that practical assistance is not required. You will not find her condoning the rudeness of ladies who reject having doors opened for them on the ground that they have the strength to perform this task themselves.

Offers to be of service in this world may not be required of etiquette, but they are not unappreciated by etiquette, either. Unless, as in this case, they are just plain silly.

REJECTING FOOD

DEAR MISS MANNERS—A friend took me to lunch, and we ordered the same entrée. She liked it; I simply did not. Since it was not the fault of the restaurant, I felt I had no right to ask for another choice (at my own expense, of course). I ate most of it, but I really did not enjoy it. Could I properly have done anything else? What if one is dining alone in that situation?

GENTLE READER—If you are dining alone, you may buy twelve dishes, if you like, and leave them all untouched. You will probably have a difficult time assuring the staff that everything really is all right, but provided you do not attempt to blame the restaurant for your changes of mind, you will not have committed an error of etiquette. (Returning spoiled or mis-cooked food is, however, not only proper but even a courtesy to the restaurateur, who will want the chance to redeem the cook's reputation.)

The situation is quite different when you are someone's guest and she feels responsible for your enjoyment. You cannot decently say, "I don't like the dinner you bought me, so I'll buy one myself."

Just eat it, will you? How you behave is more important than what you eat. Anyway, how bad can food be, when it is of your own choice and you acknowledge it to be properly cooked? If you are gracious, perhaps your friend will want to invite you out again and then you can order something different.

REFUSING DRINK

DEAR MISS MANNERS—When one is dining at a restaurant where wine glasses are already set out at each place, is it proper to turn over the glass if one does not want to be served wine? Given the same situation, is it proper to turn over the coffee cup if one does not wish coffee?

GENTLE READER—How about turning over the plate if one is not hungry? Or the butter dish if one is worried about cholesterol? Or the entire table, if one is finished and doesn't want to be offered dessert?

Miss Manners will now endeavor to get a grip on herself and acknowledge that yes, she has heard of the practice of refusing drink through the symbolic use of the table setting. She is also aware that it requires some fancy eye-work to anticipate any possible pourings and head them off with a shake of the head.

Nevertheless, that is the proper way to refuse drink. One should be able to do it once and for all the first time the waiter comes around with the bottle, simply by saying, "I won't be having wine." With coffee, this can be established by answering the inevitable question, "Regular or decaf?" by saying, "Neither, thank you."

CHILD-REARING-IN-PROGRESS

DEAR MISS MANNERS—When my wife and I took our 13-month-old daughter and my wife's mother to lunch at a fairly nice restaurant, my wife and I shared our food with our daughter by placing small portions in front of her on the table and letting her eat with her hands, as usual.

Later, my wife's mother said that we should have been more considerate of other patrons at the restaurant who may have been disgusted by our daughter's eating off the table with her hands. I should add that our daughter was very well behaved, that the restaurant was nearly empty and that we had a secluded table.

Furthermore, she said she thinks that most people would be disgusted by this, but that she herself wasn't. However, my wife thinks that not only was her mother upset over how we feed our baby in a restaurant, but also how we feed her at home. As a result, while my wife's mother is visiting, our baby is being fed spoonful by spoonful.

Now, I think that it is silly for others to get upset at a perfectly well-behaved 13-month-old who eats with her hands in a restaurant. For crying out loud, she's only 13 months old. After a fairly tense discussion about it, we agreed to let you arbitrate:

1. Are most people disturbed by babies who eat with their hands, in or out of restaurants?

2. What if they are? Isn't this a case of the problem being with them, and not with us?

GENTLE READER—Miss Manners was going to give you a gentle answer to the first question until she saw the second one. People who take the attitude that disgusting others is the problem of the disgusted, not the disgustor, should not be entrusted with the delicate task of civilizing a 13-month-old child.

Yes, you should be considerate of the feelings of others. But more important, you should be considerate of the welfare of your child, who will be ill equipped for the world if she does not learn the consequences of disgusting other people.

She also ought to be learning how to eat, for crying out loud. The time-honored method is to feed a very small child until, understandably impatient with this indignity, the child demands the privilege of wielding a spoon in order to feed herself. Admittedly, she will wield it all over the landscape until she gets the hang of it. But by presenting a utensil as the only alternative to mealtime passivity, you create a powerful incentive to begin learning table manners.

Your method not only skips this but deprives your daughter of one of life's earliest exercises of power: banging a spoon on a plate and driving the adults crazy.

More and more people are taking their children to "nice" restaurants these days, and more and more, others are objecting—not because they hate children, but because the hope of civilized dining is one reason they sought out the restaurant in the first place. You will find that people are much more tolerant of child-rearing-in-progress (such as a child who is attempting to use a spoon, while attending parents provide mop-ups and stop any outbursts, including spoon-banging) than of the encouragement of savagery that you offer.

The person who seems to be behaving best in this is your mother-in-law. She has confined herself to delicate hints, blaming others and professing not to be revolted herself.

READING AT THE TABLE

DEAR MISS MANNERS—I am a single woman who often travels alone for business and pleasure. I am stumped for a ladylike occupation to fill in the time between ordering a meal and its arrival. I have experimented with writing personal letters at the table. Will this behavior put me entirely beyond the pale, even if I use black ink and white paper?

GENTLE READER—Miss Manners is afraid that it will. For a solitary diner, reading is permissible behavior; writing is not. Do not attempt to find any logic in this distinction, because there isn't any.

WORD PROCESSING AT THE TABLE

DEAR MISS MANNERS—Is the Miss Manners laptop ban based on the laptop being a party pooper, or keeping a table for too long without just compensation, or both? Does it apply if the restaurant has no tablecloths, e.g., cafeterias, pizza houses, canteens in libraries, fast-food outlets?

I get a lot of paperwork done if I take my computer to a cafeteria and work for long stretches (during non-peak hours) while getting numerous refills of the plate and cup.

Supplementary Activities

Hard as it is on people who grew up doing their homework while eating, watching television and talking on the telephone, the only proper activity to accompany social eating is conversation. Newspapers are permitted at family breakfast, and those dining alone are allowed one slender volume, but printouts, laptops, earphones, beepers, telephones, television sets and other distractions do not belong in the dining room, much less on the table.

GENTLE READER—Miss Manners loves it when the possible applications of a seemingly simple etiquette rule require that it be turned into a full judicial opinion. All right, here goes:

The ideas behind the laptop ban are, first, that one does not do business in a place where others are engaged in the ritual of dining and, second, that one does not ignore one's table companions. Both rules also apply to telephones and paperwork, but the first does not exclude reading, which is not obviously business and makes no noise if you don't turn the pages too roughly.

Etiquette is not concerned with the table turnover and so leaves it to the individual establishment to decide whether it wants to allow postmeal lingering—which might be considered picturesque and hospitable during slow periods—or doesn't want to because it can otherwise do more business. The polite person wouldn't even attempt to keep a table when others are obviously waiting, but a restaurateur is not impolite for inquiring whether someone using the place as an office wants anything else or is ready to leave.

Considering all these requirements of etiquette and those of the restaurant business, half-empty fast-food restaurants, coffeehouses and other convenience feeding stations would be the only places where lone diners could use their laptops.

SINGING AT THE TABLE

DEAR MISS MANNERS—Why were we always told not to sing at the table? Of course, were I to do so, dreadful gastrointestinal consequences could ensue. But what was ever considered rude about it?

GENTLE READER—In the popular effort to nullify etiquette by citing exaggerations it never intended and then ridiculing them, someone is going to wax indignant about this rule. But it is not there to suppress a hymn or anthem or even a jolly old drinking song before or after eating.

You were probably told not to sing at the table because you were humming tunelessly when you were supposed to be finishing dinner, driving everybody else at the table crazy. Or crazier, by revealing to them a mouth with food in it.

Or providing irrelevant entertainment. The only proper mealtime activities for those sitting at the table (Miss Manners doesn't care for background music, but will raise no etiquette objection if Handel wants to play while others eat) is conversation. Thus singing is banned along with reading, watching television, word processing, telephoning and constructing buildings from vegetables.

FORTUNE TELLING AT THE TABLE

DEAR MISS MANNERS—Something peculiar occurs when a gentleman who occasionally takes me out to dinner orders fish or a small bird. He blows the bones into his closed fist, shakes them like dice, then throws them onto the bread plate.

Is there anything I could say to him without hurting his feelings to amend the bone behavior?

GENTLE READER—How about "Tell me my future"?

Miss Manners doesn't want to alarm you, but what you have there is not a gentleman, but an ancient soothsayer. Gentlemen do not cast bits of their dinner around like dice.

LEAVING THE TABLE

Dear Miss Manners—When two (or more) females are at a restaurant table, with or without men, if one excuses herself to go to the ladies' room, does the other excuse herself also, to accompany her?

Gentle Reader—How is that again? Are you asking whether ladies who dine together must make a unanimous decision about whether and when to go to the bathroom?

Why, no. When one lady gets up, it is certainly common for one or all the ladies present to say, "I believe I'll join you." That way directions only have to be asked once, there's a chance to talk over the gentlemen in private and the ladies can render one another assistance in seeing if dresses are straight in the back.

But this camaraderie is not required, for heaven's sake. In its own modest way, etiquette may be in the business of regulating human conduct for the general welfare, but it does allow anyone who doesn't need a diaper changed (or to change one) to go to the bathroom by herself.

LEAVING THE TABLE TO SMOKE

Dear Miss Manners—When we began our "club"—a group of 12 women friends getting together for dinner and birthday celebrations—only one member didn't smoke and there were no ordinances prohibiting smoking in restaurants. Well, the times have changed. Now five of us don't smoke and restaurants restrict smoking to the bar or prohibit it entirely.

We nonsmokers are often left at the table while the smokers go out to smoke. They sometimes get busy visiting and do not return after one cigarette. Are we wrong to feel slighted? Should we sit and wait for their eventual return, or must we join them?

Should we ask for a group discussion on this or ignore it? After half an hour, can we leave or order dinner? The last time there were just two of us nonsmokers waiting and after 45 minutes we left—not in a huff, but just tired of waiting. Now the smokers are angry with us. This doesn't seem fair, but I suppose we were wrong to leave.

GENTLE READER—It is one of the great advantages of a club that it can make rules. Etiquette rules. Made by mutual agreement, so that nobody's feelings are hurt.

All it takes here is for you to inquire pleasantly, "What should we do about waiting around while people go out to smoke? Would you say a 20-minute disappearance rule, after which others are free to leave? Ten minutes? Thirty?" Provided there are no rude cracks made about smoking, in which case you have a Miss Manners award for unusual restraint, a group of old friends surely ought to be able to make such a decision to everyone's satisfaction.

GROOMING

DEAR MISS MANNERS—Is it improper to apply lipstick at the table of a restaurant after one finishes a meal? I'm not referring to putting on additional makeup, or combing one's hair—just adding lipstick. My husband objects to this, but I have seen it done time and again in numerous types of establishments. I have been married for over 20 years and this has been a constant issue when we are dining out. Should one seek the privacy of the ladies' room to touch up? I will refrain until I receive your response.

GENTLE READER—Miss Manners is flattered at your deference to her wishes. But if she were your husband, she might wonder why, in 20 years of marriage, it has not occurred to you to offer a similar courtesy to him. After all, Miss Manners does not have to eat with you.

In fact, she has revoked the rule (developed in the 1920s when using makeup became respectable but before the mascara wand was invented) that a dab of lipstick or powder could be applied at the table, precisely because this offends many people.

HEALTH AIDS

DEAR MISS MANNERS—My boyfriend and I were out for dinner in a restaurant and he used a nasal spray while at the table. He tried to be discreet by slumping in his chair and turning his head. Would it not be proper etiquette for him to go and do this in the washroom? Besides the fact that this is a store-bought spray, not prescription, he feels that it is a necessity and that therefore he should be able to use it in a public place.

GENTLE READER—Miss Manners doesn't much care for watching people spray things up their noses, especially at mealtime, and neither, she gathers, do you. This should be sufficient reason for the gentleman to refrain from doing it, even if it were not obvious that we are not alone in this prejudice.

But she is interested in his reasoning, or rather rationalizing. Since when does the fact that a bodily function is necessary mean that it is all right to do it at the dinner table? Think about that one for a minute, since your appetite is gone anyway.

BUSING

There is a new eating rule that sounds like preparation for a legal career, where the popular byword is "You eat what you kill." But this version of the principle of self-sufficiency is slightly more considerate of others.

It is: "You clean up what you mess up." This applies to school lunchrooms, food courts, fast-food establishments and all snacking at home. Busing one's own mess is, in fact, a major contribution that such places have made to etiquette.

Leaving dishes for others to clean, a legacy from the time when all restaurants operated at a sedate pace and just about everyone even in America either had a servant or was one (or treated the lady of the house like one), can no longer be taken for granted. When Miss Manners wonders at the mad dash to be charged a lot of money for being neglected, if not snubbed, she remembers that pretentious restaurants do not actually make their patrons scrape the plates.

The polite person keeps ever alert for the necessity of cleaning up after having eaten. In a public accommodation the requirement is not subtly hidden. "Stack trays here" signs and a dirty look from subsequent diners looking for an appetizing place to settle themselves ought to be sufficient clues. One need only give careful attention to the particular system being used to know whether everything gets dumped together or should be neatly sorted.

DEPARTING

DEAR MISS MANNERS—When you are invited to a restaurant for dinner and you have chatted for a while, does the hostess or the guest suggest that you leave?

GENTLE READER—Both. The hostess says, "Would you like anything else?" when it is obvious to all that nothing further can be required until breakfast. The guest replies, "Oh, no, thank you, this has been delightful." When the bill has been paid, everybody stands up. The next thing you know, you are out the door.

A weary guest can also say "Well, this has been delightful" heartily and often enough for the hostess to get the idea that it is over.

CHECK GRABBING

DEAR MISS MANNERS—I have a relative who, when invited to dinner at a restaurant, sometimes picks up the check in spite of the fact that the inviter has acted as hostess, recommending dishes, ordering the wine, etc. In one case a large group was involved and the hostess was embarrassed. Is it proper for this guest to pick up the check despite the earnest protests of the nominal hostess?

P.S. Gender has nothing to do with this.

GENTLE READER—It is hard to believe that a generous act could be rude and Miss Manners trusts that your relative does not intend this to be so. Nevertheless, that is its effect.

There are occasions when check squabbling is permissible, even expected, among relatives. For example, a young adult with some limited income ought to attempt to pay checks for older relatives, even though they both know that the older people should seldom allow it. Never to allow reciprocity, and to undermine a hostess's position by assuming her right, is offensive. Miss Manners suggests that when next you entertain this person in a restaurant, you instruct the waiter beforehand that he is not to accept her payment.

SPLITTING THE CHECK

DEAR MISS MANNERS—At a birthday party in a restaurant attended by a group of friends, a heated discussion erupted over how the luncheon bill should be paid. When one woman brought out her credit card and said, "Let's just have the restaurant divide the bill by three, and we'll each add our share of the tip," the honoree protested that this was a low-class way of paying and most inconsiderate to the restaurant. She said the correct way was for this day's hostess (a rotating position) to pay the entire bill and then to send the other two women a bill for their share.

A third woman chipped in with "It is unmannerly to show money on the table." She refused to use her credit card and wrote a check instead. The matter was never settled. Each woman ended up paying as she chose, and it was agreed that in the future the hostess would decide how the bill was to be paid. I am asking if there is an approved procedure that would be considered good manners.

GENTLE READER—Unmannerly to take out money to pay a restaurant bill? Inconsiderate to the restaurant to divide up the bill? What on earth do you people think a restaurant is?

Miss Manners knew there was some odd restaurant idolatry going on, but this is ridiculous. A restaurant is a business that sells cooked food and table service. While it may be unseemly for a group of friends to argue over who ate what, the mere fact of dividing a bill and paying it with money or a credit card applies to all classes except the criminal ones.

UNEXPECTEDLY SPLITTING THE CHECK

DEAR MISS MANNERS—A couple we have known for years called and said, "We are taking you out to dinner. Which restaurant do you prefer?" My husband and I didn't care for either place they then named, but we figured if they're paying, it's their choice.

After a meal that seemed to be comprised of industrial waste, the waiter presented the check to the husband who gave it to his wife, who then said to me, "Your half is $55 if we divide it in half."

We hadn't been expecting to be hit up for half the check and did not have the cash. I told our alleged hostess to give me her half in cash and I'd put the entire check on a credit card. She appeared miffed and said we'd earn extra frequent flyer miles at her expense. What is the proper reaction and decorum for such an unsavory display of bad manners?

GENTLE READER—Miss Manners suggests you take your frequent flyer miles and use them to escape from these people.

It's not that they muddled their invitation. There is plenty of confusion these days between entertaining at restaurants and merely offering to meet at restaurants, but "We are taking you out to dinner" is not ambiguous. These people clearly stated that they were taking you out to dinner, and then didn't.

What is worse is their attack on your morals. Accusing friends of greed and fraud strikes Miss Manners as even worse a violation of friendship than stiffing them with a bill they didn't expect. Miss Manners hopes you did not pretend to be amused at this insult. You should merely have said quietly, "I'm sorry, but I misunderstood you when you asked if you could take us out to dinner, and this is the only way I can cover the bill."

WHAT AND WHEN TO TIP

The principles of tipping are always the same: 15 to 20 percent of the bill, never anything under 50 cents for the most trivial service, no tips to owners of establishments, even if they also do work that would ordinarily require tipping, and no fair withholding tips in situations when they are customary. Bad service should be reported to management when it happens, which is before the bill is presented.

Every once in a while, Miss Manners goes over these rules and forces herself to listen afterward to the objections of those who like the idea of rewarding and punishing (as long as their own wages are not reduced when they have a bad day) and of owners of service establishments who declare that they would be only too happy to be insulted by tips.

The truth is that Miss Manners finds the whole subject of tipping distasteful. Because tips are an institutionalized portion of many people's income, it is unforgivable to withhold them, but we would all, including the tax collectors, be better off if service costs were built into all bills.

Q: *Would you consider a 20 percent tip in a restaurant flashy and vulgar?*

A: Only if it is accompanied by the statement "Here you are, my good fellow."

Q: *When you are someone's guest in a restaurant, is it appropriate for that person to also leave the tip, or should the guest take care of the tip?*

A: The host tips, because he does not show the bill to the guest, who therefore doesn't know what to tip.

WHERE TO TIP

DEAR MISS MANNERS—What I do not know about tipping (and I doubt that I am alone) is what to *do* with the tip. Do I hold it in my hand so the person can pick it up? Do I place it in the outstretched hand? Do I put it somewhere where it can be picked up? At what point is the tipping done? What if I am caught with nothing between a $50 bill and a nickel? Or what if I have only a credit card? I tend to avoid going to places where there are people who have to be tipped so I will not suffer the embarrassment of doing it wrong. Can you help?

GENTLE READER—Surely there are few areas of etiquette in which the subjects cooperate more readily in making the gesture easy. If there is not an outstretched hand, there will be when you place money into yours and reach out. Restaurant tips are left on the table, or marked on the credit form.

If you do not have the cash available for a tip, say so. Say, "I'd like to give you something for your trouble," and then ask where you can change a $50 bill or cash a check. A bill for which someone could reasonably be expected to have change, say $10, can be handed over with the remark, "Could you please give me $9 change for this?"

BENEFIT OF THE DOUBT

DEAR MISS MANNERS—Do customers have the right to deprive a waitress of a tip if they catch her cheating on the bill? Since I look older than I am, I believe this is being done to older people.

GENTLE READER—Miss Manners understands that you have worked yourself up into believing that you have a class-action case, which you are going to settle by, in effect, docking the offenders' wages. She begs you to calm down and remember, first, that people must be given the benefit of the doubt and, second, that tipping has nothing to do with crime and punishment. Waitresses do not cheat on bills; they make mistakes. When this is drawn to their attention, they apologize and correct their mistakes.

PRIVATE ENTERTAINING

"POTLUCK"

Miss Manners remembers when the charmingly homely phrase "We're having potluck" meant, "We're always so happy to see you that we aren't going to limit it to times when we do formal entertaining. You're practically a member of the family, and if you don't mind sharing our humble daily fare, you'll always be welcome, so please come and take your chances."

What it means now is something more like, "We're willing to see you, but we consider it too much trouble to make any effort on your behalf and we're certainly not planning to stand the cost of feeding people just because they happen to be our guests. If you come, you must bring your own provisions, or at least enough of one dish so that you and the other people who are going to be here can all be fed without our having to do anything more than place our orders. Surely if we let you gather in our house, we are contributing enough."

So potluck is now bad luck for anyone who had expected to be treated as a guest and an even greater misfortune for the noble institution of hospitality.

At this point, Miss Manners would dearly like to avoid hearing tedious accounts of how busy everybody is. As she spends all her time languidly draped on the porch swing, waiting for someone to come along and set the thing in motion, she can't be expected to understand what it is to have a life. But there is something important she doesn't seem to be able to make others understand. That is that sharing refreshment with others is a sacred duty, from which constraints of money and time do not excuse anyone. The literature of religions is filled with stories about a god who appears in disguise, to the everlasting glory of the poor who graciously share their last crumb, and to the eternal shame of the rich who tell him that he should have brought a dish for potluck and money for the cash bar.

By consigning the modern potluck dinner to the garbage pail of spoiled ideas, Miss Manners is by no means condemning the idea of cooperative entertaining. Even for those

Conscripted Cooks

"Potluck" is supposed to be an ingratiating apology for serving simple food to last-minute guests, not a clever way for people to order free carryout food under the pretense of giving a dinner party to feed the cooks.

Except at cooperative gatherings (in which the person who provides the site has no greater say in the plans than anyone else), hospitality means offering people refreshment, not assigning them to deliver it. The guests' proper contributions consist of being charming, thanking the hosts in writing and eventually returning the invitation. They may choose to send flowers or bring wine or nonperishable foods such as candy, but no such offering is required and they should not expect it to be added to the meal.

who do not brag about how busy they are, cooperative dinners can be a delightful way to provide variety and convenience in informal socializing. There is, for example, a tradition of cooperative picnics, evening meetings, and dinners among groups that meet on a regular basis.

The distinction is that a potluck event has a host and a cooperative event doesn't; it only has an organizer, who is usually the person at whose house it takes place.

Hosts provide refreshments. They get to decide the terms of the occasion all by themselves, are responsible for providing everything and are compensated only by the happiness, gratitude and future reciprocal hospitality of their guests. Organizers, in contrast, issue suggestions, rather than invitations, and have to consider counter-suggestions. They arrange for whatever is needed by asking people what they want to bring (making sure to offer the choice between cooking and buying items) and assign themselves to contribute whatever they identify as lacking. Although this task is generally rotated, nobody gets social credit for having entertained, because everyone has done so equally. Nobody has to write thank you letters.

Miss Manners hopes it will be noticed who is left out of these descriptions. It is the person who says, "Please come to dinner," and when the guest accepts, envisioning a pampered evening of being entertained, adds, "and bring dessert for 16 people." It is also the person who carries it one step further by kindly volunteering to be guest of honor, as well as ersatz host. "We're getting married and we're having a potluck reception, so I'll let you know what you're supposed to bring," such a person announces. Or "I'm celebrating my birthday and everybody should bring a favorite dish." Or "We want to go to a nice restaurant to celebrate our anniversary and it will be about $50 a person." That is because Miss Manners is throwing such people out of society.

Miss Manners often hears from the unfortunate targets of these people, who find that they have accepted an invitation to cook and sponsor a party they hadn't planned to give, and probably to bring the host a present besides, not to mention thanking him for his kindness. She hereby sets these victims free. If they are to be hosts, they can enjoy the advantage of hosts, which is to spend the evening at home. Naturally, they must be polite when saying that they are so sorry, they will be unable to attend after all. But if the guest of honor finds that he is left to do the job of honoring himself alone—well, Miss Manners hates to be harsh. But potluck to him.

AN EXTREME CASE

DEAR MISS MANNERS—When my sister invited me and my two children for Christmas dinner and informed me that our parents and other relatives would be in attendance, I asked her what I could contribute to the occasion. She quickly assured me that she was preparing a very special meal and that I was not to bring any food items—but that I would be expected to pay $50 if I wished to attend!

I'm sorry to say that I paid Sister Scrooge the money. My parents were visiting from out of town and I dearly wanted to spend Christmas with them. To my further dismay, I discovered that Mom and Dad were also charged $50, as was my sister's mother-in-law!

The dinner was mediocre and most everything came straight out of a can. My sister is quite comfortable financially and I find this meal charge simply appalling. How can I express my feelings of disgust to her and still maintain family harmony?

GENTLE READER—Hold on a minute, please, while Miss Manners tries to deal with her own feelings. They are not harmonious. They are not even presentable.

Your sister sold Christmas dinner to her own family? And then she cheated them by substituting cheaper goods than she had advertised?

All right, that's it. Miss Manners has had enough holiday spirit. She doesn't see how you can mention this decently; the only way to keep family harmony would be to refrain from mentioning it to your sister at all. But you would be well advised to arrange another family dinner for the next occasion. Otherwise the rates are likely to go up and the quality down.

UNSOLICITED DONATIONS

DEAR MISS MANNERS—Guests often ask if they can bring something when I have eight or ten people to dinner, but I enjoy planning the entire meal and using my good china, silver and place cards. (When it is potluck, or a picnic, I welcome a dish to serve.)

Often guests will bring a bottle of wine or a plant, but twice a guest has arrived with her special dessert for the dinner. This is awkward for me. I do not wish to upset my guest, but it does mean another complete set of dishes to be brought out at the last minute. Should this surprise dessert be served along with mine, after my dessert, or later in the evening? What would you do?

GENTLE READER—Miss Manners is afraid that what she would have done, had you simply stated the problem, would not have been as good as one of your suggestions.

Miss Manners would just have thanked the dessert-maker and put the dessert away for future use, in the freezer if necessary, saying, "We'll think of you when we enjoy this." This is the standard way of accepting wine that one does not want to serve with the meal for any number of reasons (including the fact that guests never bring enough of it to go around a whole dinner party).

Although they mean well, guests simply cannot show up with a surprise replacement for the menu. They can bring presents to be used at the hosts' discretion, but not ones that obviously require last-minute alterations in the dinner plans. Your idea of serving the dessert later in the evening, after your own dessert—with coffee in the living room, for example— will make the point somewhat better. "Oh, I can't possibly; I'm stuffed," your guests will say, with more truth than charm.

THE GUEST'S OBLIGATIONS

Any social life beyond a spur-of-the-moment supper or excursion to the movies is impossible without guests' taking a serious attitude toward invitations. So Miss Manners does not want to hear any more about what guests don't have to do "nowadays."

Do you ask your car every morning whether it expects you to give it gas "nowadays" just because you want it to take you somewhere? The real question for nowadays is how much prodding and nagging the hosts can politely do.

Guests should, of course, answer telephoned or written invitations definitively and immediately. Not only does Miss

Manners abhor "response cards," but those who use them report that they aren't working anyway. Delinquent guests are probably picking off the stamps to put on their bills, presuming they even recognize that they are still expected to pay their bills nowadays. As "R.s.v.p." (upper- and lower-case) is no longer eye-catching even on formal occasions, Miss Manners suggests the formal alternative: "The favour of a reply is requested."

Social invitations are neither transferable nor enlargeable. A host wanting to know if the guests are part of a couple, or allowing them to form one for the evening, should ask for a name and send that person an invitation. Miss Manners has even invented a written form: an enclosed card saying, "If you would like us to invite an additional person, please give us the name and address." Just putting "and guest" or "and escort" is insulting to known couples and intimidates those who then feel they can't go alone.

An implicit, and certainly an explicit, dress standard should be followed. Hosts should indicate sensibly what they expect, while those who wish their guests to appear as jokes should specify that the occasion is a costume party.

Accepting an invitation means agreeing to meet whichever other people the hosts have seen fit to invite and to make do with whatever refreshments are provided, skipping what is unsuitable, even if it means eating beforehand. It is hospitable to provide enough variety that those with the commoner dietary restrictions—vegetarians, dieters, non-drinkers, observers of religious requirements—will have something, if not everything there, to eat.

Miss Manners does not know how one mandates a general attitude of cooperation among guests, even if it is only to the extent of declining the invitation so that they don't have to be bound by other expectations. If she were to allow the command about taking things seriously, she knows, sadly, what the reaction of those guests would be:

"Do you think this applies to us?"

"Nah."

STARVING FOR DINNER

DEAR MISS MANNERS—My husband and I were invited to my friend's house at 5:00 to eat, but my husband came home from work at 4:00, starving. He wanted me to call her and see if we could come over then, but I wouldn't. How would you have handled this?

GENTLE READER—With a sandwich.

PLACE SETTINGS: A REVIEW

It's a sad commentary on the state of modern manners that the dinner table is regarded less as a succulent scene than as a social booby trap. What *is* all that stuff?

Miss Manners sometimes ponders such a question herself, but only in regard to the food. Between today's adventurous cooks and analytical eaters, there's some weird-looking stuff appearing.

Everything else on the table is just equipment to eat it with, along with a few decorative touches. That shouldn't be frightening. It's designed to feed you, not test you. And it's supposed to be appetizing, not off-putting. This is why although originality counts, it usually counts against. Digestion being a complicated enough process, everything on the table should be decipherable.

It is all very well to spend hours constructing centerpieces of tiny golf courses with living grass or chase scenes made with the children's action figures, but there is a great deal more to be said for flowers, and even more for fruit, which can be eaten afterwards, or instead of the sweet dessert, for that matter. (Notwithstanding people who oddly respect the chastity of parsley and garnishes carved to look like flowers, all food that appears on the table is considered fair game, as it were.)

Candlesticks should appear only after dark, when their presence is explicable. Napkin rings, however whimsical, should be used only when necessary to identify napkins for reuse by householders or houseguests. Salt, in shakers or more formally in cellars with wee spoons, should be within reasonable reach. Ashtrays now serve the purpose of dividing the diners into opposing, enraged camps, which is why they have entered peacetime service as candy or nut dishes. Menu stands, however, should have a new lease on life, as they enable people to forage for food to which they have no moral, religious, medical or philosophical objections. Place cards not only mean that the hosts' memories will not be taxed in telling guests where to sit, but that guests who have forgotten one another's names can sneak a quick look and strangers who fall in love at the table can write their telephone numbers on them.

In the basic setting, you probably know that the plate in front of you and the napkin on it are yours. But there seems to be some confusion about what is farther afield, and one person going in the wrong direction can throw off an entire table. The glasses assigned to you are on your right, and you may plop bread or salad—not both unless you like oily bread—on any little plates you find on your left at informal meals.

The flatware issue is the emotional one, Miss Manners realizes, although she has never understood why. Most pieces give at least a hint of their function—the salad fork has a cutting edge on the side and the fish knife has a bone-picking point on the end—but in any case, they are all sensibly lined up in the order they should be used.

Forks are put on the left, in strict outside-to-inside order of use; their matching knives are in the same order to the right; and first-course utensils—soup spoons or oyster forks—are to the right of the knives. Anything above the plate is dessert silver, its handles facing in the direction from which it would have traveled had it gone upwards from plate-side, with spoon placed above fork or knife.

So what's the problem? People who run out of silver prematurely don't arouse the hostess's scorn—only the worry that she set the table wrong or that she should install a metal detector by the door as the guests leave.

Miss Manners hopes she has made all this sound as easy as pleasant eating should be. But not so much so that the concept of practicality is thrown back in her face, an unseemly procedure at table. No, no, no, you cannot put mustard jars, pickle bottles, cream containers, packages of crackers, boxes of cereal, plastic honey or syrup bottles, take-home covered food trays, Chinese carry-out cartons, pizza boxes, or any other commercial container on any table. Not if you want to consider yourself civilized.

Never mind that this is the fast, sensible, easy, practical way to serve things. Miss Manners has been talking about setting a table, not a trough.

FACE DOWN

DEAR MISS MANNERS—I recently read, in a novel, "When silver is embossed on the back (forks and spoons) you are supposed to let it show." They were turned face down at the table.

I have been to a lot of social events in my 65 years and I have never seen this done. Is it correct?

GENTLE READER—Yes, it is, but Miss Manners finds that she then also has to turn face down at the table. This is to avoid seeming to laugh at the expressions of those who believe the table to be set upside down, as it were. The mixture of pure horror with the determination not to be rude by seeming to notice that one's host has done something appalling by usual standards does them credit. It is also understandable. Engraving silver on the back is a European custom, not an American one, which is why they and you are surprised to see it.

THE WRONG FORK

DEAR MISS MANNERS—At a dinner party for ten people, there were placed in front of each, three forks, three knives and four teaspoons. I picked up a fork to have my salad and the host screamed over the table, to my utter embarrassment, "Jim, you picked up the wrong fork!" I felt awful. I think it was in bad taste. Do you agree?

GENTLE READER—Yes, but what do you expect of people who think that teaspoons belong on the dinner table?

Correcting the table manners of a guest is a violation of etiquette greater than anything one can do with a fork, short of stabbing one's host in the throat with it. What makes it a particularly heinous offense is the unfortunate general belief that etiquette arbiters exist—that, indeed, etiquette exists—purely for the purpose of humiliating others.

CANDLES

DEAR MISS MANNERS—Because of these perilous times, older people no longer have the option of traveling freely about the cities at night, so therefore we must do our entertaining during daylight hours.

I know that in the safer days of yesteryear, it was decreed that lighted candles should not be used in decorations during daylight hours. The aged who are captives in our own homes after darkness falls are only able to have parties at a time when, according to these tenets, candles should not be lit.

But we need all the joy and happiness we can find, and lighted candles flickering merrily in a centerpiece on the serving table at a brunch could give such a life to our day. If a change would cause discomfort or embarrassment, then of course it should not be considered. But where is the harm? Why cannot a custom be changed to accommodate the times and add joy to the lives of deserving people?

Can you not please bring countless experiences of delight to those of us who can no longer be safe going to parties at night and decree that we, too, may have the pleasure of lighted candles at our daytime parties? You will do us a great service if you will.

GENTLE READER—Miss Manners feels trapped. She would have to have a heart of stone to rebuff your sweet and reasonable plea—and yet even she cannot turn day into night.

You could make the same argument on behalf of wearing evening clothes to breakfast.

Allow her to make you an offer.

Of course go ahead and light your candles. As you point out, this is not an etiquette rule designed to protect people's feelings, which would therefore cause hurt if it were broken. Yet it is a rule, all the same, based on giving a certain orderliness to the day. Candlelight is not needed during daylight. And your guests, like you, have a lifetime of observing this rule.

So just do Miss Manners the favor of saying, when you light up, "I thought we could enjoy candlelight even though it's daytime." This would reassure your guests that you are breaking the rule for a reason, and not out of confusion.

SEATING (PART ONE)

DEAR MISS MANNERS—Our dining room table has three side chairs to a side, plus an arm chair at each end. What is the correct seating arrangement when there are four or six people at the table? Does one remove the unused chairs to the wall, or leave them in place?

GENTLE READER—Once upon a time, four was considered the minimum number of places to set at a table, even when fewer people were dining. This has little to do with your question. Miss Manners is mentioning it because she is the last person on earth who remembers this, and she has gotten tired of waiting for a suitable question in which to use this choice piece of information. She keeps the practice alive herself, only to the extent of having a minimum of four chairs at the table, but does not actually set phantom covers for fear of guests' murmuring, "Well, she's finally crossed the line."

Now, you were asking about genuinely extra chairs, above the magic number. Yes, they go against the wall. At a very long table, it would be awkward to have only one person at each side with the hosts far away at the ends. Four people can be grouped with the host (or hostess) at one end, and one guest to one side and two (or one and then the host) to the other. Or you can have two people on the middle of each side, facing each other. Six can usually spread out enough to use the table conventionally, but it is also permissible not to use the ends, or to use only one of them.

SEATING (PART TWO)

DEAR MISS MANNERS—My son gave a dinner party, inviting me, another young man and his mother, and a young lady with her mother. Exactly how should we have been properly seated at the table?

GENTLE READER—Seating arrangements are the jigsaw puzzles of the etiquette trade. Miss Manners just loves looking at all the odd pieces, with their different configurations, and then making them fit perfectly.

The characteristics to be noted separately (as if to separate out the edge pieces) are gender, relationship, age and degree of intimacy. But as each person has more than one of these (like puzzle pieces that have both bits of sky and bits of ground), it is not obvious how to place them. Except, of course, to Miss Manners.

Your son, as host, goes at one end of the table. He could

put you at the other, as stand-in hostess; but if he were, for example, engaged to the young lady, or if she had substantially helped him with the occasion, he might have her take the hostess place, which would put you in precedence after the two other mothers (because as family, you come after the other ladies of your generation) but before the other young gentleman (because you are a lady). If the other young gentleman was a co-host, he could have been in that place.

The two other mothers go on either side of your son, the elder to his right, and never mind how he's supposed to know which one that is. The young lady goes next to the young man's mother, which would also put her next to you if you are hostess; you would go there if she were hostess. And the young man goes between the young lady's mother and the hostess. Note that you get to check out both of your son's friends this way. You didn't really come there to meet other mothers.

By the way, Miss Manners is puzzled that you put this request after the party, thus suggesting that you were unsatisfied with the seating. Please don't be hard on the boy. You should be proud that he gives dinner parties and not expect him to be as good at puzzles as a Grand Master like Miss Manners.

PLACE CARDS

DEAR MISS MANNERS—How are place cards properly used? I have about 150 guests for a wedding breakfast and would like to make specific seating arrangements. How do I direct the guests from the receiving area outside the ballroom to the proper tables?

May I have a handwritten menu displayed at each table? If

so, how is it done? How are the napkins folded? At most ho-
tels, I have seen them stuffed in the stemware, but I don't like
the look of it.

GENTLE READER—Miss Manners is afraid that in order to
explain the proper use of place cards, she must begin with
the improper use of place cards. After much thought about
who would be best off next to whom, the hosts properly place
them at each place (you begin to see the origin of the name).
Then a guest who doesn't care a fig for the overall plan but
is merely trying to sit next to a particular person sneaks in
and moves them.

Thwarting the place-changers is a side benefit of notifying
guests where they are to sit before they enter the dining room.
This can be done by using a chart (prettily done so it doesn't
look like a sales chart left over from the previous booker of
the room) or leather holders (in the shape of the table, with
name cards stuck around them). Or it can be done by giving
each guest a tiny envelope designating his or her table (the
process by which gentlemen are notified of their dinner part-
ners at a formal dinner).

At the table, the place card is put either above the plate or
on top of the napkin, which is, in turn, on top of the place
plate. This is one good reason for not stuffing the napkins in
the wine glasses; another is that they look stupid there.

The menu can be put in a menu stand if you haven't already run up too much of a bill at the stationer's, what with
leather seating charts and tiny gilt-edged envelopes. It is also
proper merely to place the menu itself between two place settings, to be shared by two people whose heads bumping together may eventually lead to another wedding.

TYPES OF SERVICE

At stake is the question of whether formal meals should be offered around on platters, with guests taking what they want, or whether each guest should be handed a prefilled plate, with some of everything on it. The teams are Russian, French, American (known to the English as English) and Restaurant, listed in reverse order of probable popularity. All of these are types of formal service, in the modern sense of meaning that guests do not actually have to bus their own dishes.

In French service, huge numbers of dishes are set out in symmetrical patterns on the dining table, guests being expected to help themselves and one another from what they find within reach. Standard until the late nineteenth century, this may be said to survive in today's buffet table. How we evolved to being dumber than the Victorians, who realized how foolish it was to ask human beings to eat standing up, Miss Manners cannot say.

In Russian service, which replaced the French, food is arranged on platters that are taken around to the seated guests, who serve themselves. Leaving enough to go around depends on the honor system. In formal American service, the only service that still honors the noble and ancient ritual of personally carving for one's guests, the host or hostess carves the meat at the table after inquiring about the preferences of each guest. If the vegetables are put on too, and if everyone passes the plates down the table (and, if they are overly polite, all the way around and back again), it is "family style," but if servers do all that, it is formal.

Only in Restaurant service, which is to say at all except the truly best restaurants, is food "plated" in the kitchen and each person given some of everything. The commercial attraction is that this is the speediest service and employs the fewest people. Miss Manners considers that neither attractive nor practical, it being the only service in which guests are not allowed to choose what and how much they want.

FOOD SELECTION

We all agree that everybody does not eat everything. That is not the issue. There are polite rules for avoiding what you don't want:

1. If you are serving yourself, from a tray or a buffet table, don't take it. Take what you can eat and leave the rest.

2. If you are given something you don't eat, mess up the plate a bit (sure, you know how—Miss Manners saw you hiding your vegetables under your potatoes when you were a mere toddler).

3. If your list of things you don't eat covers everything served at a normal meal, then eat before you go out. Take a minimum amount for messing-up purposes. We don't want to waste food, but we don't want to waste the hosts' energies, either, by making them rush around trying to find something to please you.

4. If you are worried about truly hidden ingredients—ubiquitous foodstuffs that are not easily detected but to which you have a serious reaction—you are allowed one whispered word to the hosts, or a reminder in advance to those with whom you dine often. Other than that, follow rules one through three.

5. Don't discuss food. (If Miss Manners weren't so polite, she would say, "For heaven's sake, shut up about it.") Nobody is interested in hearing about what you don't eat. Don't announce it, and refuse to be led into any discussions about it.

If prodded, just smile happily and decline what is offered, refusing to supply an explanation.

Miss Manners is fighting this battle for the sake of belea-
guered hosts, so she feels she must make her own requests of
them, in their interest:

1. Use service that allows people to choose what they want
to eat. These include the formal presentation of a platter by
a waiter, or the informal passing of platters from guest to
guest. In family-style service, the host should look inquisi-
tively at the guest he is about to serve, allowing for that person to say, "I prefer dark meat," or "No meat for me, please."

2. Serve generous amounts of the foods most people are
likely to eat: salads, vegetables and fruits.

3. Pretend not to notice what your guests are eating or not
eating. If Miss Manners can get them to be quiet about it, that
is the least you can do. It is the height of rudeness to monitor what your guests choose to put in their mouths.

SAYING GRACE

DEAR MISS MANNERS—Is it appropriate to have grace said at
a dinner party where the guests are of mixed faiths? I say it
should be reserved for family or religious occasions. Could you
enlighten me?

GENTLE READER—There is nothing wrong with saying grace
at any meal, provided one does not use the opportunity to enlighten the guests more directly about one's religious beliefs.
Those of another faith or custom may merely observe a respectful silence.

BEGINNING WHEN SERVED

DEAR MISS MANNERS—Will you please repeat that it is OK to begin eating when one is served, rather than waiting for a full table to be served, with cold plates for those who were served first. When I quote you, people think I am making it up.

GENTLE READER—Miss Manners said it all right, but you must have been under her dinner table at the time. What she said was "Oh, please go ahead and start" to her own guests, as gracious hostesses do when they don't have enough footmen to serve everyone at once. Gracious guests, however, must unfortunately sit looking as if food were the last thing on their minds until the hostess takes the first bite of a course or until they hear these magic words.

CLINKERS

DEAR MISS MANNERS—They told me to ask you. They said you know everything. Is it actually necessary to touch glasses when making a toast? I've been sitting at a table with six or eight people when someone offers a toast. Then we all go around the table clinking glasses with everyone else. Why not just raise the glass and glance around the table?

GENTLE READER—Miss Manners likes your attitude. She also likes your approach. Clinkers should indeed confine themselves to those within easy clinking distance.

FORCE-FEEDING

DEAR MISS MANNERS—I thought I would vent my feelings to you instead of killing my neighbor who, like my sister and a close friend, keeps trying to force-feed me. These are the ploys I keep encountering:

"Oh, but it's not sweet." (Of course it's sweet; it's dessert, isn't it?)

"This isn't cake—it's bread." (This doesn't change its nature. And whoever came up with the idea that if something has one single ingredient that might be good for you—bananas, cranberries, apricots—it's legitimate to call it bread?)

"But I baked it especially for you because I was so sure you'd like it. Just try a little piece." (This is obviously manipulative, and is often used by the two who are considerably heavier than I.)

"Oh, but if you don't order dessert, I can't either." (Nonsense! Don't pretend I'm depriving you.)

"Oh, but how can the rest of us eat it in front of you when you're not having any?" (Double nonsense! If you enjoy it, eat it. How could it bother me to watch you eat something I don't want?)

Why is it so easy to remember that Mary is a vegetarian, Karla keeps kosher, Sandra is diabetic, Marcia is allergic to chicken and Sue doesn't care for seafood—and not realize that I don't like desserts?

I know which of my friends don't take cream and sugar in their coffee and I don't offer it to them. If I slip up, they say those magic words, "No, thank you," and I say, "Oh, that's right; I forgot." I don't say, "Oh, please try just a little! It's low-fat! It isn't sugar; it's sweetener. But I bought it especially for you because I know you don't like real cream. Oh, dear, then I can't have any in my coffee!"

Why doesn't a simple "No, thank you" work? I have to be so adamant in refusing that I sometimes feel rude, even though they are really the ones being rude by insisting.

The Ultimate Test

The most difficult of all etiquette rules has nothing to do with forks. It is to refrain from drinking a toast to yourself. When champagne is being served, everyone else has a raised glass and you are every bit as proud of yourself as they are, it is tempting, but wrong, to join their tribute. The correct thing is to smile modestly until they take a sip and then get your own drink by delivering your own return toast to them.

GENTLE READER—Saying "No, thank you" does work. But like child-rearing, it may have to be repeated for 20 years before it gets through.

Miss Manners is even more exasperated by these attempts at force-feeding than you are, if you can imagine such a thing. This is because those who practice it, in ways you so vividly describe, believe they are being polite.

It is polite to provide bountifully for the pleasure of one's guests. But to push their faces into it is not polite. Only parents of minors and working physicians and nutritionists are supposed to take an interest in what goes into other people's mouths, and even they are not allowed to issue instructions while out socially.

Miss Manners is afraid you just have to keep repeating your polite refusal. It may not be understood, but your failure to engage in a conversation about the matter by offering support to your refusals will eventually bore even the most persistent person.

TALKING FOOD TO DEATH

DEAR MISS MANNERS—Would you kindly shine some light on the annoying habit of talking the food to death at the table? I have become increasingly reluctant to share a meal with my sainted mother, because of the conversation about ingredients, texture, temperature, portion size, preparation time, comparisons with "last time I fixed it," ad nauseam. I lose my appetite.

GENTLE READER—There used to be a rule against any discussion of food at the table, and mellow old Miss Manners relaxed it just enough to allow people to give compliments.

Now she's sorry. Mothers aren't so difficult. You can always distract them by asking advice. But the food fusses are going to drive us all mad.

RESISTING PROVOCATION

DEAR MISS MANNERS—After several years as an ovo-lacto vegetarian (I don't eat any flesh, including fish and chicken, but I do eat milk, cheese and eggs), it is obvious that I am well-nourished and that I cannot inflict my special orders on host-esses. I eat a light snack before a dinner party, and then eat whatever is served that is not meat.

Hostesses often respond to this by rushing into the kitchen to bring me hunks of cheese, or by being offended that I won't even taste the main course. How can I make it clear that I am not going to starve, and that I am enjoy-ing part of the meal and all the hospitality? Is it rude not to tell the hostess one's eating habits? Is it rude to accept an in-vitation to dinner, knowing that meat will probably be served?

How do I deal with people who want to know all the de-tails of my diet? It's not that I object to promoting vegetari-anism, it's just that there is a risk of generating very unpleasant dinner conversation. People don't really want to hear that their veal cutlet is unhealthy and that the calf was subjected to numerous atrocities before slaughter.

GENTLE READER—Miss Manners deals in etiquette atrocities and she is outraged that you are being subjected to two of the most common current ones: being goaded to eat and being goaded to talk about your eating habits. The sort of people who do this mistake force-feeding for hospitality and inter-rogation for conversation. Of course you can accept dinner invitations, but Miss Manners wishes you would get them from a better sort of people.

To maintain your admirable politeness in the face of such provocation is not easy. You need to keep demurring in such a blandly polite way as to make them give up the struggle. "No, you're very kind, but I really don't care for anything more, thank you. No, really. Please don't get up, I really don't want anything more." And if the cheese is brought anyway, Miss Manners advises you to ignore it.

"Oh, I don't want to bore you with my private habits. No, really. If you're interested, give me a call sometime. This is nei-ther the time nor the place for such a discussion." Then open another topic.

FIRE!

Dear Miss Manners—When I put a very hot piece of food in my mouth by mistake, as seems to happen so much more frequently now that microwaves are common, is there any way out besides swallowing it and burning my mouth? I can't see taking food out of my mouth in the presence of others.

Gentle Reader—To sacrifice the interior of your mouth for the sake of etiquette is an honorable way to go, but even Miss Manners does not recommend martyrdom when there is a reasonable way out.

The customary procedure is to keep the food in the mouth, while making assorted yelping grunts and wild gestures, including pointing to the mouth. Miss Manners cannot say that she endorses this. Nor is it of much practical help.

The Fire Department method is better. This is to grab the nearest glass of water and drown the offending item. The fact that the water glass may be someone else's is overlooked on the grounds that this is an emergency. But as you rightly understand, it is not so much of an emergency as to allow spewing the food indignantly over the tablecloth.

SECOND HELPINGS

DEAR MISS MANNERS—When and how should the hosts offer seconds at a small, informal dinner party (four to 14 people around one table), and when and how may the guests ask to be served a second helping of a course? I have seen every variation, from the host individually asking each guest, to the host not mentioning the subject and the guests asking if they may have seconds. What if, for example, the guest is aware that there is more meat in the kitchen that the host probably intends to offer but has forgotten?

Assuming there is more to be served, what should a good host do? And, failing a direct offer, what may a hungry guest do by way of saying, "Please, sir, may I have some more?"

GENTLE READER—While hosts may always offer seconds, guests must proceed more cautiously because they can neither be sure whether more is available nor how many other courses are going to be served.

Except your particular guest, of course. Miss Manners notices that this guest has taken the precaution of checking out the supplies in the kitchen. Such prudence doesn't count.

Perhaps the hosts are having a whole other dinner party the following night.

A host may say, "Would you like some meat?" as many times as he pleases and as long as the larder holds out (although the terms "seconds" and even "some more" are not used, lest it seem as if he is keeping track). A guest can only prompt by saying repeatedly, "My, that was good," not by quoting Mr. Dickens.

CLEANING THE PLATE

DEAR MISS MANNERS—When dining out, should some food always be left on the plate, or should everything on the plate be eaten? Weight-watching, dieting, food prejudices, religious restrictions and the like are not the problem. Proper etiquette is, and I would like a ruling.

GENTLE READER—Funny you should ask. The question of purposely leaving food on the plate happens to be intimately bound up with Miss Manners' own history.

It used to be required. Supposedly, one left enough to show that far from being shortchanged at mealtime, one had been amply supplied. The rule was stated as "Leave something for Miss Manners" (in England, "Leave something for Lady Manners").

Never mind the picture that suggests of poor Miss Manners, going around slopping up everybody's leftovers. Even if she tried, she couldn't stuff them all in, which meant that good food was going to be thrown away.

This is not an attractive idea and Miss Manners didn't want to be responsible for it. Rather, she aligned herself with the grandmother of a fellow etiquetteer, Eleanor Roosevelt.

"My grandmother came to believe," Mrs. Roosevelt wrote in *Eleanor Roosevelt's Book of Common Sense Etiquette,* "that food was needed in the world and we who had an abundance should not waste it. Then I was cautioned never to take more on my plate than I could eat!" Thus the Clean Plate Club was formed. It may contribute its own problems, but at least they pertain only to the eater and not to the rest of the world. And they can't be blamed on Miss Manners.

LEFTOVERS

DEAR MISS MANNERS—I always prepare extra food when inviting guests, so I will have enough left over for my family the next day. After dinner, a guest asked me for a plate of food to take home for her meal the next day. I was surprised, but fixed a plate. Does this happen often?

GENTLE READER—Miss Manners certainly hopes not, but she has learned not to discount the likelihood of achieving new lows in human behavior.

She might even be unwittingly abetting the spread by publishing such examples as you mention. There could be people reading this and saying, "What a great idea! I could make my hosts prepare me a doggie bag."

It is, of course, a highly improper request—and yet another instance of people confusing private homes with public restaurants, where the request to take leftovers home is not unreasonable. It is, for example, equally shocking but more common for guests to decide at the last minute whether to attend, to bring along their own friends, and to announce their food likes and dislikes as if their friends' homes were public accommodations.

Unless you had reason to believe that your friend had no other hope of being fed the next day (and those so destitute need longer-term help; but one is not likely to find them at dinner parties), you should have politely refused. Cooperating with rude demands only encourages people to make more of them. "I'm so sorry, but I can't" would be all you had to say.

CLEANING UP

The reason for that moment of silence at the end of all but the most formal festive dinners is not that people slip into a happy reverie of gratitude for the wonderful meal they have been served, or for the delight of gathering with their relatives and friends. It is not even that the digestion process is working in such high gear as to render the mind inoperable, although this may be a contributing factor.

Miss Manners knows what it is. At half the jolly dinner tables the following thoughts are being framed and unsuccessfully telegraphed across the ravaged platters.

Host: "Why are they all just sitting there? Do they think I'm their servant? Don't they realize I've been slaving away all day to make this dinner? Now that they've all got their faces stuffed, can't they manage to haul themselves to their feet and do something useful?"

Each guest: "Why aren't we being asked to leave the table instead of just sitting here? Do they expect us to clean up? I didn't come over here to work. Nobody helps me when I entertain. Why can't we just leave everything and go find some more comfortable chairs?"

At the other half of the tables, the thoughts are somewhat different:

Host: "I suppose if I get up, they'll all traipse into the kitchen after me and make a mess. Why don't they just let me get things done instead of interfering with the way I like to do things? The last time I let people help, it took me twice as long to clean up, what with their stacking things all over the place, dumping everything that didn't belong there down my garbage disposal, putting my good knives in the dishwasher and putting things away so that for weeks afterward I couldn't find anything."

Each guest: "Now we're going to get the martyr act and be told to go enjoy ourselves while all the work of cleaning up goes on, or this mess is left to congeal on the table. If everybody pitched in, we could all get it done in no time and continue the party in the kitchen, instead of sitting around being made to feel guilty."

Uncharacteristically, Miss Manners refuses to declare one attitude right and the other wrong. At formal dinner parties, guests are not pressed into service, and hosts without household help are supposed to be able to deliver persuasively the following announcement: "Please just leave it. Everything will be taken care of—just come and join me in the living room."

At informal meals, guests may be allowed to do minor tasks, such as helping clear; and at family gatherings, they may do serious tasks. It is all up to the hosts, some of whom appreciate help, perhaps to the point of sulking when there isn't enough, and some of whom hate it. Similarly, some guests hate doing it and others hate sitting there being waited on.

There shouldn't be an etiquette problem here. Miss Manners should just solve the situation by mixing and matching, so that the right hosts get the right guests. Never mind if that breaks up family groups. Because of this issue, they weren't getting along so well together, anyway.

Nevertheless, it may not be practical. Therefore, Miss Manners must train people in how to determine which group they are in and pack them off to do her proud. Since the decision about accepting help is the host's, those attending dinners in households where the guests outnumber the footmen must offer to help. This is done by asking a straightforward question: "What can I do to help?" The proper accompanying gesture is essential. One can neither hop up and start grabbing things nor lean back with folded arms and dead eyes. One must lean forward and smile eagerly, an expression that is aided by imagining that the issue is not whether one can help but whether one can go home now.

The host must make a clear reply. "Oh, that's all right—I'll manage" means "yes"; the guest who hears it must rise and request further instruction. "No" is expressed by "Please don't—I have my own system and I really prefer to do it myself." The guest who hears that may safely return to the business of digestion.

TAKING HOME THE FLOWERS

DEAR MISS MANNERS—I just learned that it is the custom among some people to decide with the other guests seated at their table which of them will take the centerpiece when he or she leaves the party. This seems wrong on at least two accounts: the flowers are the property of the hosts, and the containers might well be valuable or belong to someone else. Is this proper behavior? And if not, how does the gentle hostess keep her flowers on her table?

GENTLE READER—By inviting people who are there to enjoy her hospitality, not to swipe things to feather—or flower—their own nests.

Miss Manners is just barely aware that some people actually ask their guests to take home the flowers, if there are more than they can use themselves and they have not arranged to send these to a charitable organization. Fine. They can also offer guests the tablecloths and the silverware, if they so choose.

But guests cannot simply walk off with anything except the food in their tummies. Miss Manners does not think it unreasonable to expect guests to focus their attention on participating in the occasion they are attending, rather than planning how to dismantle it for their private enjoyment later.

A PERFECT DINNER PARTY

DEAR MISS MANNERS—When my mother turned 80, my brother hosted a dinner party for her in a suburban hotel. He sent out hand-addressed, engraved invitations about a month before the party.

Miraculously, 65 people accepted and 65 came for dinner. (One woman who had accepted called three days beforehand to say she could not come because of a health problem and one man came without having replied to the invitation.) No uninvited children were brought by their parents.

My brother graciously paid the whole bill, asking no one—guest or sibling—for any contribution.

The invitation did not say "No gifts," and when guests asked if we were collecting money, we told them gifts were not expected. Some did bring gifts and Mother sent out all her thank you notes in the next two weeks.

The balloon bouquets were beautiful. The food was wonderful. The service was good. The piano player was delightful. The company was convivial. All had a wonderful time and will remember this birthday party fondly for the rest of their lives.

I thought you might like to know that some people still know how to behave.

GENTLE READER—Like to know? Miss Manners has been clutching this letter to her bosom, saving it to remind herself that there is hope yet ahead.

INDEX